Be Reconciled!

TEXTS BY POPE JOHN PAUL II
Edited and arranged by
Seamus O'Byrne
with a Foreword by
✠ Donal Murray

VERITAS PUBLICATIONS

First published 1985 by
Veritas Publications
7-8 Lower Abbey Street
Dublin 1

ISBN 0 86217 235 7

Designed by Liam Miller
Typesetting by Printset & Design Ltd., Dublin
Printed in the Republic of Ireland

LIST OF CONTENTS

EDITOR'S NOTE

The text of this book has been taken from the English language edition of the *Osservatore Romano (O.R.)* with the permission of the Libreria Editrice Vaticana. The material, arranged in chronological order, is presented here as an aid to sermons and instructions on the Sacrament of Penance.

Thanks are due to all those who helped in its publication

Seamus O'Byrne

FOREWORD

In his first encyclical, Pope John Paul II pointed out that Jesus meets the people of every time, including your own, with the same words, "You will know the truth, and the truth will make you free". All through his pontificate, he has been concerned to stress that there can be no authentic human freedom which is not based on the whole truth about God, about humanity, about the world.

Sin is always a kind of falsehood: it involves acting as though things were not as they are, as though God did not exist, as though other people did not matter, as though I were omnipotent. That falsehood leads inevitably to slavery. Freedom means the ability to deal with reality; it is undermined by a refusal to recognise reality. Sin is a search for salvation where it can never be found; it is the pursuit of illusions. The Holy Father has warned about many of the dead-end paths which lie temptingly open to the people of today - the paths that seek salvation through possessions, through technological advance, through sexual licence, through ideologies and economic systems. The goods of the earth, human sexuality, the possibilities of science and technology are all gifts of God, but they are not God himself. To turn them into idols is to destroy their true meaning and to deprive them of their purpose in God's plan.

It is not surprising, then, that the Sacrament of Penance plays so large a part in the addresses and writings of Pope John Paul II. It is a sacrament of truth and freedom, which undoes the falsehood and the slavery of sin. This book comes at a particularly appropriate time, since 1983-84, with the celebration of the Jubilee Year of the Redemption and the meeting of the Synod of Bishops on the theme of "Reconciliation and Penance in the Mission of the Church", focused the attention of the whole Church on the topic and provided the occasion for many statements by the Holy Father which it is good to have so easily available.

The Sacrament of Penance is an acknowledgement of the whole truth, and a reception of the gift of genuine freedom which is promised to the children of God. It acknowledges the truth about God. Only in the light of that truth can sin be recognised for what it is. As a liturgical act, Penance is, first and foremost, a prayer, praising, thanking and adoring God. The focus of attention is on God rather than on ourselves. At the same time, the sacrament is an offering by God, through the ministry of the Church, of that mercy which is stronger than sin.

The Sacrament of Reconciliation is also a community act, an act of the Church. It involves recognising that sin is never a merely private affair, but always harms the whole Body of Christ and its mission in the world. At the same time it is an expression of the anxiety of the whole Church to lead its members to conversion. There is, rightly, today an increasing realisation of our social responsibility for the evils around us and of our calling not only as individuals but as a community to work for the coming of the kingdom of justice, peace and love. Services of Penance, whether non-sacramental or with individual confession and absolution, have a powerful part to play in fostering a sense of solidarity in the struggle against falsehood and slavery and in the acceptance of God's gifts of truth and freedom.

The sacrament is, finally, an acknowledgement of the truth about oneself. The Holy Father has been particularly insistent on the fact that renewal must begin in the hearts of individuals. Without that personal repentance, the community aspect could all too easily be reduced to a complaint that "they" should do something about it. That would be an escape from responsibility. There is no "they", only "us", only individuals who practise, or tolerate, or turn a blind eye to, or give up the struggle against the evils that are around us and within us. That is why the concrete acknowledgement of the truth about one's own personal sinfulness is the first step in building a renewed and renewing community.

Like all the sacraments, Penance is linked to the Eucharist, the great and central sacrament. The celebration of the Eucharist ought to awaken a need for Penance, and Penance is a preparation for gathering in truth and freedom as the Eucharistic community.

Fr Seamus O'Byrne is to be congratulated for providing us with this comprehensive collection of the Holy Father's teaching on this subject which is so central to Christian living. The preaching of Christ began with the call to "Repent", and "believe in the Gospel". May this book help many people to hear that call more clearly and may it contribute to the renewal and revitalisation of the Church in truth and freedom as we approach the beginning of the third millenium of the Christian era.

✠ DONAL MURRAY

Address to a Group of Canadian Bishops

17 November 1978

At this moment in the life of the Church there are two particular aspects of sacramental discipline that are worthy of the special attention of the universal Church, and which I wish to mention, in order to assist bishops everywhere. These matters form part of that general discipline of which the Apostolic See has prime responsibility, and in which the Pope wishes to sustain his brethren in the episcopate and to offer a word of encouragement and pastoral orientation for the spiritual well-being of the faithful. These two matters are the practice of first Confession before first Communion and the question of general absolution. After some initial experimentation had been conducted, Paul VI in 1973 reiterated the discipline of the Latin Church in regard to first Confession. In a spirit of exemplary fidelity numerous bishops, priests, deacons, religious, teachers and catechists set out to explain the importance of a discipline which the supreme authority of the Church had confirmed, and to apply it for the benefit of the faithful. Ecclesial communities were comforted to know that the universal Church gave renewed assurance for a pastoral matter in which, previously, honest divergence of opinion existed. I am grateful to you for your own vigilance in this regard and ask you to continue to explain the Church's solicitude in maintaining this universal discipline, so rich in doctrinal background and confirmed by the experience of so many local Churches. With regard to children who have reached the use of reason, the Church is happy to guarantee the pastoral value of having them experience the sacramental expression of conversion before being initiated into the Eucharistic sharing of the Paschal Mystery.

As Supreme Pastor, Paul VI manifested similar deep solicitude for the great question of conversion in its sacramental aspect of individual Confession. In an *ad limina* visit earlier this year he referred at some length to the Pastoral Norms governing the use of general absolution

(Address of 20 April 1978 to Bishops from the United States), showing that these norms are in fact linked to the solemn teaching of the Council of Trent concerning the divine precept of individual confession. Once again he indicated the altogether exceptional character of general absolution. At the same time he asked the bishops to help their priests "to have an ever greater appreciation of the splendid ministry of theirs as confessors... Other works, for lack of time, may have to be postponed or even abandoned, but not the Confessional". I thank you for what you have done and will do to show the importance of the Church's wise discipline in an area that is so intimately linked with the work of reconciliation.

In the name of the Lord Jesus, let us give assurance, in union with the whole Church, to all our priests, of the great supernatural effectiveness of a persevering ministry exercised through auricular confession, in fidelity to the command of the Lord and the teaching of his Church. And once again let us assure all our people of the great benefits derived from frequent Confession. I am indeed convinced of the words of my predecessor Pius XII: "Not without the inspiration of the Holy Spirit was this practice introduced into the Church" (AAS 35, 1943, p. 235).

O.R. 557   30 November 1978

Encyclical Redemptor Hominis 4 March 1979

"Let a man examine himself, and so eat of the bread and drink of the cup" (*1 Cor 11:28*).

This call by the Apostle indicates, at least indirectly, the close link between the Eucharist and Penance. Indeed, if the first word of Christ's teaching, the first phrase of the Gospel Good News, was "Repent, and believe in the gospel" - *metanoiete* - (*Mk 1:15*), the Sacrament of the Passion, Cross and Resurrection seems to strengthen and consolidate in an altogether special way this call in our souls. The Eucharist and Penance thus become in a sense two closely connected dimensions of authentic life in accordance with the spirit of the Gospel, of truly Christian life. The Christ who calls to the Eucharist banquet is always the same Christ who exhorts us to penance and repeats his "Repent". Without this constant ever-renewed endeavour for conversion, partaking of the Eucharist would lack its full redeeming readiness to offer God the spiritual sacrifice in which our sharing in the priesthood of Christ is expressed in an essential and universal manner. In Christ, priesthood is linked with his Sacrifice, his self-giving to the Father; and precisely because it is without limit, that self-giving gives rise in us human beings, subject to numerous limitations, to the need to turn to God in an ever more mature way and with a constant, ever more profound conversion.

In the last years much has been done to highlight in the Church's practice - in conformity with the most ancient tradition of the Church - the community aspect of penance and especially of the Sacrament of Penance. We cannot however forget that conversion is a particularly profound inward act in which the individual cannot be replaced by others and cannot make the community be a substitute for him. Although the participation by the fraternal community of the faithful in the penitential celebration is a great help for the act of personal conversion, nevertheless, in the final analysis, it is necessary that in this act there should be a pronouncement by the individual himself with the whole depth of his conscience and with the whole of his sense of guilt and of trust in God, placing himself like the Psalmist before God to confess: "Against thee, thee only, have I sinned" (Ps 50(51):4). In faithfully observing the centuries-old practice of the Sacrament of Penance - the practice of individual confession with a personal act of sorrow and the intention to amend and make satisfaction - the Church is therefore defending the human soul's individual right: man's right to a more personal encounter with the crucified forgiving Christ, with Christ saying, through the minister of the Sacrament of Reconciliation: "Your sins are forgiven" (Mk 2:5); "Go, and do not sin again" (Jn 8:11). As is evident, this is also a right on Christ's part with regard to every

11

human being redeemed by him: his right to meet each one of us in that key moment in the soul's life constituted by the moment of conversion and forgiveness. By guarding the Sacrament of Penance, the Church expressly affirms her faith in the mystery of the Redemption as a living and life-giving reality that fits in with man's inward truth, with human guilt and also with the desires of the human conscience. "Blessed are those who hunger and thirst for righteousness, for they shall be satisfied" (*Mt 5:6*). The Sacrament of Penance is the means to satisfy man with the righteousness that comes from the Redeemer himself.

O.R. 573   19 March 1979

Address to Students   10 April 1979

My sons and daughters, you have pointed out at your Congress the sufferings and the contradictions by which a society is seen to be overwhelmed when it moves away from God. The wisdom of Christ makes you capable of pushing on to discover the deepest source of evil existing in the world. And it also stimulates you to proclaim to all men, your companions in study today, and in work tomorrow, the truth you have learned from the Master's lips, that is that evil comes "out of the heart of man" (*Mk 7:21*).
So sociological analyses are not enough to bring justice and peace. The root of evil is within man. The remedy, therefore, also starts from the heart. And - I am happy to repeat - the door of our heart can be opened only by that great and definitive word of the love of Christ for us, which is death on the Cross. It is here that the Lord wishes to lead us: within ourselves. All this time that precedes Easter is a constant call to conversion of the heart. This is real wisdom: "Fear of the Lord is the beginning of wisdom" (*Sir 1:16*).

Beloved sons and daughters, have, therefore, the courage to repent; and have also the courage to draw God's grace from sacramental Confession. This will make you free! It

12

will give you the strength that you need for the undertakings that are awaiting you, in society and in the Church, in the service of men. The true service of the Christian, in fact, is qualified on the basis of the active presence of God's grace in him and through him. Peace in the Christian's heart, moreover, is inseparably united with joy, which in Greek (*chara*) is etymologically akin to grace (*charis*). The whole teaching of Jesus, including his Cross, has precisely this aim: "that my joy may be in you, and that your joy may be full" (*Jn 15:11*). When it pours from a Christian heart into other men, it brings forth hope, optimism, and impulses of generosity in everyday toil, infecting the whole of society.

O.R. 578   23 April 1979

Homily: Phoenix Park, Dublin
29 September 1979

The call to conversion in the Eucharist links the Eucharist with that other great Sacrament of God's love, which is Penance. Every time that we receive the Sacrament of Penance or Reconciliation, we receive the forgiveness of Christ, and we know that this forgiveness comes to us through the merits of his death - the very death that we celebrate in the Eucharist. In the Sacrament of Reconciliation, we are all invited to meet Christ personally in this way, and to do so frequently. This encounter with Jesus is so very important that I wrote in my first Encyclical Letter these words: "In faithfully observing the centuries-old practice of the Sacrament of Penance - the practice of individual confession with a personal act of sorrow and the intention to amend and make satisfaction - the Church is therefore defending the human soul's individual right: man's right to a more personal encounter with the crucified forgiving Christ, with Christ saying, through the minister of the sacrament of Reconciliation: 'Your sins are forgiven''; 'Go, and do not sin again''. Because of Christ's love and mercy, there is no sin that is too great to be forgiven; there is no sinner who will be rejected. Every person who repents will be received by Jesus Christ with forgiveness and immense love.

It was with great joy that I received the news that the Irish Bishops had asked all the faithful to go to Confession as part of a great spiritual preparation for my visit to Ireland. You could not have given me a greater joy or a greater gift. And if today there is someone who is still hesitating, for one reason or another, please remember this: the person who knows how to acknowledge the truth of guilt and asks Christ for forgiveness, enhances his own human dignity and manifests spiritual greatness.

I take this occasion to ask all of you to continue to hold this Sacrament of Penance in special honour, for ever. Let all of us remember the words of Pius XII in regard to frequent Confession: "Not without the inspiration of the Holy Spirit was this practice introduced into the Church" (AAS 35, 1943, p. 235).

Dear brothers and sisters: the call to conversion and repentance comes from Christ, and always leads us back to Christ in the Eucharist.

O.R. 602   8 October 1979

Address to the Bishops of the USA
5 October 1979

As bishops who are servants of truth, we are also called to be servants of unity, in the communion of the Church. In the communion of holiness we ourselves are called to conversion, so that we may preach with convincing power the message of Jesus: "Reform your lives and believe in the Gospel". We have a special role to play in safeguarding the Sacrament of Reconciliation, so that, in fidelity to a divine precept, we and our people may experience in our innermost being that "grace has far surpassed sin" (*Rom*

5:20). I, too, ratify the prophetic call of Paul VI, who urged the bishops to help their priests to ''deeply understand how closely they collaborate through the Sacrament of Penance with the Saviour in the work of conversion'' (Address of 20 April, 1978). In this regard I confirm again the norms of *Sacramentum Paenitentiae* which so wisely emphasize the ecclesial dimension of the Sacrament of Penance and indicate the precise limits of general absolution, just as Paul VI did in his *ad limina* address to the American Bishops.

Conversion by its very nature is the condition for that union with God which reaches its greatest expression in the Eucharist. Our union with Christ in the Eucharist presupposes, in turn, that our hearts are set on conversion, that they are pure. This is indeed an important part of our preaching to the people. In my Encyclical I endeavoured to express it in these words: ''The Christ who calls us to the Eucharistic banquet is always the same Christ who exhorts us to penance and repeats his 'Repent''. Without this constant and ever-renewed endeavour for conversion, partaking of the Eucharist would lack its full redeeming effectiveness'' (*Redemptor Hominis, 20*). In the face of such a widespread phenomenon of our time, namely that many of our people who are among the great numbers who receive Communion make little use of Confession, we must emphasize Christ's basic call to conversion. We must also stress that the personal encounter with the forgiving Jesus in the Sacrament of Reconciliation is a divine means which keeps alive in our hearts and in our communities, a consciousness of sin in its perennial and tragic reality, and which actually brings forth, by the action of Jesus and the power of his Spirit, fruits of conversion in justice and holiness of life. By this sacrament we are renewed in fervour, strengthened in our resolves and buoyed up by divine encouragement.

O.R. 605   29 October 1979

Letter to the Diocese of Rome 22 February 1980

Lent is not only a reminder, but a continual summons. To enter this period and live it in the spirit handed down to us by the most ancient and still living tradition of the Church means: *to open one's own conscience.* To let Christ himself open it with the word of his Gospel, but above all with the eloquence of his Cross.

Lent is, therefore, an exceptional opportunity to save in each of us "the inner man" (*Eph 3:16*), so often forgotten, who, thanks to the Passion and the Resurrection of Christ, is created "in true righteousness and holiness" (*Eph 4:24*).

Let not this time pass for us without the Sacrament of Penance, without the examination of conscience, without repentance for our sins and at the same time the resolution to improve; let it not pass without confession and absolution.

The Christ of Lent is he who, from his Cross, in his Passion and Death, utters, in a way, God's supreme last word of love for man, the love of the Father for the prodigal son. Only this love is creative; only it has the power to save man and the world.

Let us not remain indifferent to it. Let us try to respond to it. Let us seek this response in our heart. Let us seek it in the life of the Church in the course of this Lent.

O.R. 622   3 March 1980

Letter on the Eucharist   24 February 1980

In the Encyclical, *Redemptor Hominis*, I have already drawn attention to the close link between the Sacrament of Penance and the Sacrament of the Eucharist. It is not only that Penance leads to the Eucharist, but that the Eucharist also leads to Penance. For when we realize who it is that we receive in Eucharistic Communion, there springs up in us

16

almost spontaneously a sense of unworthiness, together with sorrow for our sins and an interior need for purification.

But we must always take care that this great meeting with Christ in the Eucharist does not become a mere habit, and that we do not receive him unworthily, that is to say in a state of mortal sin. The practice of the virtue of penance and the Sacrament of Penance are essential for sustaining in us and continually deepening that spirit of veneration which man owes to God himself and to his love so marvellously revealed.

We find in recent years...that sometimes, indeed quite frequently, everybody participating in the Eucharistic assembly goes to communion; and on some such occasions, as experienced pastors confirm, there has not been due care to approach the Sacrament of Penance so as to purify one's conscience. This can of course mean that those approaching the Lord's Table find nothing on their conscience, according to the objective law of God, to keep them from this sublime and joyful act of being sacramentally united with Christ. But there can also be, at least at times, another idea behind this: the idea of the Mass as only a banquet in which one shares by receiving the Body of Christ in order to manifest, above all else, fraternal communion. It is not hard to add to these reasons a certain human respect and mere ''conformity''.

This phenomenon demands from us watchful attention and a theological and pastoral analysis guided by a sense of great responsibility. We cannot allow the life of our communities to lose the good quality of sensitiveness of Christian conscience, guided solely by respect for Christ, who, when he is received in the Eucharist, should find in the heart of each of us a worthy abode. This question is closely linked not only with the practice of the Sacrament of Penance but also with a correct sense of responsibility for the whole deposit of moral teaching and for the precise distinction between good and evil, a distinction which then becomes for each person sharing in the Eucharist the basis for a correct judgement of self to be made in the depths of the personal conscience. St Paul's words, ''Let a man examine himself'' (*1 Cor 11:28*), are well known; this judgement is an indispensable condition for a personal decision whether to approach Eucharistic communion or to abstain.

O.R. 625   24 March 1980

Homily at the Parish of St Ignatius of Antioch, Rome   16 March 1980

Lent is the time of a particularly loving expectation on the part of our Father with regard to each of us, that, even if he is the most prodigal of sons, he may, however, become aware of how wasteful he has been, confess his sin for what it is and finally turn with full sincerity to God.

This man must arrive at the Father's house. The way that leads there passes through an examination of conscience, repentance and the resolution to improve, as in the parable stages, at once logical and psychological, of conversion. When the man has experienced all these stages in himself, in the depths of his heart, the need of confession springs up in him. This need comes into conflict, perhaps, with shame, but when conversion is real and authentic it overcomes shame: the need of confession, of liberation from sins, is stronger. We confess them to God himself, although the priest-man listens to them in the confessional. This man is the humble and faithful servant of that great mystery which has taken place between the returning son and the Father.

In the period of Lent the confessionals are waiting; the confessors are waiting; the Father is waiting. We could say that it is a period of special solicitude on the part of God to forgive and remit sins: the time of reconciliation.

Our reconciliation with God, the return to the Father's house, is carried out by means of Christ. His passion and death on the cross are set between every human conscience, every human sin, and the infinite love of the Father. This love, ready to raise and forgive, is nothing but mercy. Each

18

of us, in personal conversion, in repentance, in the firm resolution to change our ways, and finally in confession, agrees to carry out a personal spiritual labour, which is the prolongation and the distant reflection of that salvific labour which our Redeemer undertook. Here is what the Apostle of reconciliation with God says: "For our sake he made him to be sin who knew no sin, so that in him we might become the righteousness of God" (2 Cor 5:21). So let us undertake this effort of conversion and repentance of ours through him, with him and in him. If we do not undertake it, we are not worthy of Christ's name, we are not worthy of the inheritance of redemption.

"Therefore, if any one is in Christ, he is a new creation; the old has passed away, behold, the new has come. All this is from God, who through Christ reconciled us to himself and gave us the ministry of reconciliation" (2 Cor 5:17-18).

O.R. 627   8 April 1980

Homily to Priests and Seminarians at Fulda
17 November 1980

The shepherd's watchful ministry... means being ready to defend others against the ravaging wolf - as in the parable of the Good Shepherd - or against the thief that he may not break into the house. With that I do not mean a priest who keeps a strict, distrustful and merciless eye on the flock entrusted to him, but a shepherd who aims to free his flock from sin and guilt by the offer of reconciliation, who above all grants the people the Sacrament of Penance.

"For Christ", the priest may and should call out to an irreconciled and irreconcilable world: "be reconciled with God" (2 Cor 5:20). In this way we reveal to the people the heart of God the Father and are thus an image of Christ the Good Shepherd. Our whole life can then become a sign and

tool of reconciliation, the "sacrament" of the union between
God and man.

But together with me you will note that the personal
reception of the Sacrament of Penance in your parishes has
fallen off very considerably in recent years. I earnestly
beseech you, indeed I admonish you, to do everything
possible to make the Sacrament of Penance in personal
confession something which all who have been baptized will
again regard as the natural thing to do. That is the aim of
penitential Church services which play a very important part
in the practice of the Church, but under normal
circumstances cannot be a substitute for the personal
reception of the Sacrament of Penance. But also endeavour
yourselves to receive the Sacrament of Penance regularly.

O.R. 662   15 December 1980

Encyclical Dives in Misericordia

30 November 1980

The Church lives an authentic life when she professes and
proclaims mercy - the most stupendous attribute of the
Creator and of the Redeemer - and when she brings people
close to the sources of the Saviour's mercy, of which she
is the trustee and dispenser. Of great significance in this area
is constant meditation on the word of God, and above all
conscious and mature participation in the Eucharist and in
the Sacrament of Penance or Reconciliation that prepares
the way for each individual, even those weighed down with
great faults. In this sacrament each person can experience
mercy in a unique way, that is the love which is more
powerful than sin. This has already been spoken of in the
Encyclical, *Redemptor Hominis*; but it will be fitting to return
once more to this fundamental theme. It is precisely because
sin exists in the world, which "God so loved... that he gave
his only Son" (*Jn 3:16*), that God, who "is love" (*1 Jn 4:8*),

cannot reveal himself otherwise than as mercy. This corresponds not only to the most profound truth of that love which God is, but also to the whole interior truth of man and of the world which is man's temporary homeland.

Mercy in itself, as a perfection of the infinite God, is also infinite. Also infinite therefore and inexhaustible is the Father's readiness to receive the prodigal children who return to his home. Infinite are the readiness and power of forgiveness which flow continually from the marvellous value of the sacrifice of the Son. No human sin can prevail over this power or even limit it. On the part of man only a lack of good will can limit it, a lack of readiness to be converted and to repent, in other words persistence in obstinacy, opposing grace and truth, especially in the face of the witness of the Cross and Resurrection of Christ.

O.R. 661   9 December 1980

Address to the Penitentiaries of the Major Basilicas   30 January 1981.

The satisfaction that this audience gives me is even greater because it takes place while the Encyclical *Dives in Misericordia* is being read and studied in the Church: from various standpoints, which are complementary with one another, your office is dedicated to the exercise of the ministry of divine mercy. The Penitentiary, furthermore, has an extremely delicate and important role in helping the Pope in his office of the keys and in the power to loose and bind. In its sphere of competence it embraces the Church in all her catholicity, without limits arising from rites or territory. The Penitentiary Fathers, furthermore, because of their origin from the most varied countries in the world, the multiplicity of the languages in which they express themselves, and because in point of fact ecclesiastics and lay faithful of the whole world trustfully turn to them, when

21

they come "to see Peter" (*Gal 1:18 Vulg.*), represent in action the ministry of reconciliation which, by the power of the Holy Spirit, as at Pentecost, is exercised on "devout men from every nation under heaven" (*Acts 2:5*).

The Penitentiary Fathers of the Patriarchal Basilicas... bear the burden of the day and the heat (*cf. Mt 20:12*) of hearing sacramental confession for long hours every day, and especially on feast days.

With the very constitution of the Colleges of Penitentiaries and with the particular norms by which, at the cost of exempting them from the customary or *ex lege* practices of their respective religious families, it consecrates them to dedicating the whole of their ministry to confessions, the Holy See intends to show with these facts the extraordinary veneration with which it regards the use of the Sacrament of Penance, and in particular the form that must be its normal one, that is, that of auricular confession. And I still remember the joy and emotion I felt last Good Friday, when I came down to St Peter's Basilica to share with you the high and humble and very precious ministry that you exercise in the Church.

I wish to say to the Penitentiary Fathers and also to all priests in the world: at the cost of any sacrifice, dedicate yourselves to the administration of the Sacrament of Reconciliation, and be certain that it forms Christian consciences, more and better than any human device, any psychological technique, any didactic and sociological method. In the Sacrament of Penance, in fact, it is God, "rich in mercy", who is at work (*cf. Eph 2:4*). And keep in mind that the teaching of the Council of Trent about the necessity of the integral confession of mortal sins is still in force in the Church, and always will be (Sess. XIV, Cap. 5 and can. 7: Denz-Schön. 1679-1683; 1707). The norm taught by St Paul and by the same Council of Trent, according to which the worthy reception of the Eucharist must be preceded by the confession of sins when one is conscious of mortal sin, is and always will be in force in the Church (Sess XIII, Cap. 7, and can. 11: Denz-Schön. 1647-1661).

Renewing this teaching and these recommendations, we

certainly do not wish to ignore that recently (cf. AAS 64 (1972) pp. 510-514) the Church has extended the use of general absolution, for serious pastoral reasons and under precise and indispensable norms, in order to facilitate the supreme good of grace for so many souls. But I wish to recall the scrupulous observance of the above-mentioned conditions and to stress that, in the case of mortal sin, even after general absolution, there exists the obligation of a specific sacramental confession of the sin, and to confirm that, in any case, the faithful have the right to their own private confession.

In this connection I wish to emphasize the fact that, rightly, modern society jealously watches over the inalienable rights of the person: how, then, precisely in that most mysterious and sacred sphere of the personality in which the relationship with God is lived, could one desire to deny the human person, the individual person of every faith, the right of a personal, unique conversation with God, by means of the consecrated ministry? Why would one desire to deprive the individual member of the faithful, who is precious as such before God, of the deep and extremely personal joy of this extraordinary fruit of grace?

I would like to add, furthermore, that the Sacrament of Penance, because of the wholesome exercise of humility and sincerity that it involves, the faith it professes in *actu exercito* in the mediation of the Church, the hope it includes, and the careful examination of conscience that it requires, is not only an instrument aimed at destroying sin - the negative phase - but also a valuable exercise of virtue, which is itself expiation, an irreplaceable school of spirituality, and a highly positive process of regeneration.... In this sense, confession, rightly instituted, is already in itself a very high form of spiritual direction.

Precisely for these reasons, the sphere of the use of the Sacrament of Reconciliation cannot be reduced to the mere hypothesis of grave sins: apart from the considerations of a dogmatic character that could be made in this connection, we recall that confession periodically renewed, the so-called confession "of devotion", has always accompanied the ascent to holiness in the Church.

I am happy to conclude by reminding myself, you Penitentiary Fathers, and all priests, that the apostolate of confession already has its reward in itself: the consciousness of having restored divine grace to a soul cannot but fill a priest with unutterable joy. And it cannot but encourage him to the humblest hope that the Lord, at the end of his earthly day, will open to him the ways of life: "those who have instructed many in virtue, as bright stars for all eternity" (*Dan 12:3*).

While I invoke on you personally, and on your delicate and meritorious ministry, the abundance of divine graces, I willingly impart to you the conciliatory Apostolic Blessing, the sign of my constant favour.

O.R. 672   23 February 1981

Address to the Bishops of Japan
23 February 1981

In my first Encyclical I devoted rather lengthy sections to two vital aspects of the Church's life: the Sacraments of Penance and the Holy Eucharist. I have repeatedly emphasized the great power of these sacraments in regard to Christian living. And today I would encourage you personally to do everything in your power to help the ecclesial community to appreciate fully the value of individual confession as a personal encounter with the merciful and loving Saviour, and to be faithful to the directives of the Church in a matter of such importance. The norms of the Apostolic See in regard to the altogether exceptional use of general absolution also take into account "a right on Christ's part with regard to every human being redeemed by him" (*Redemptor Hominis, 20*).

O.R. 674   9 March 1981

Address to the Clergy of Todi and Orvieto

22 November 1981

As is known, the Father who made us sons in Baptism remains faithful to his love, even when through his own fault man separates himself from him. His mercy is stronger than sin, and the Sacrament of Confession is the most expressive sign of this, almost a second Baptism, as the Fathers of the Church call it. In Confession, the same grace of Baptism is renewed, in fact, for a new and richer integration in the mystery of Christ and of the Church.

O.R. 712   30 November 1981

Apostolic Exhortation, Familiaris Consortio (n. 58)

22 November 1981

An essential and permanent part of the Christian family's sanctifying role consists in accepting the call to conversion that the Gospel addresses to all Christians, who do not always remain faithful to the "newness" of the Baptism that constitutes them "saints". The Christian family too is sometimes unfaithful to the law of baptismal grace and holiness proclaimed anew in the Sacrament of Marriage.

Repentance and mutual pardon within the bosom of the Christian family, so much a part of daily life, receive their specific sacramental expression in Christian penance. In the Encyclical *Humanae Vitae* (section 25), Paul VI wrote of married couples: "And if sin should still keep its hold over them, let them not be discouraged, but rather have recourse with humble perseverance to the mercy of God, which is abundantly poured forth in the Sacrament of Penance".

The celebration of this sacrament acquires special significance for family life. While they discover in faith that sin contradicts not only the covenant with God, but also the

25

covenant between husband and wife and the communion of the family, the married couple and the other members of the family are led to an encounter with God, who is "rich in mercy", who bestows on them his love which is more powerful than sin, and who reconstructs and brings to perfection the marriage covenant and the family communion.

O.R. 715   21-28 December 1981

Address to the Bishops of Abruzzi and Molise
4 December 1981

The Sacrament of Penance is the ordinary and necessary way for all those who, after baptism, have fallen into serious sin. Its scope is not limited, however, just to wiping out sins in hearts that have repented, but it is also the manifestation of the merciful goodness of God and of his glory according to the triple expression of the great Bishop of Hippo: confession of life, confession of faith, confession of praise. With this sacrament, as the Rite of Penance says in n. 7, "the Church proclaims her faith, gives thanks to God for the freedom with which Christ freed us, offers her life as a spiritual sacrifice in praise of the glory of God". It must not be forgotten, therefore, that the celebration of penance is always an act of worship in which the Church praises the holiness of God and confesses the marvels of his merciful love, which heals, raises from the dead and sanctifies.

The Church exercises the ministry of reconciliation by means of you bishops and your priests. You impart forgiveness of sins in Christ's name and in the power of the Holy Spirit. Be wise judges, able to understand personal situations and suggest the most suitable remedies; be above all fathers who reveal to men the heart of the heavenly Father. Do not fail to promote penitential celebrations for the purpose of bringing home to the faithful the Christian sense of sin and of the necessary conversion. Promote opportune initiatives aimed at reviving in Christian communities the spirit of repentance, above all in the "special" times of the liturgical year.

These celebrations may be particularly useful for children, making them aware of the true liberation brought about by Jesus. In young people, furthermore, they may develop the sense of conversion, reminding them of their commitment and making them see in it the way to the perfect freedom of the sons of God. To these latter, above all, it is necessary to bring home the importance of having a fixed confessor to whom they can habitually have recourse to receive the sacrament at difficult moments of confusion, doubt and uncertainty. The confessor, thus becoming also a spiritual director, will be able to indicate to individuals the way to follow to respond generously to the call to holiness.

Also for the sick and the old, who cannot go to church, the possibility of receiving the grace of the sacrament with a certain frequency will be a support and consolation. They will feel less the weight of illness and loneliness and will be able to unite their sufferings more generously with the redeeming passion of Christ.

O.R. 718   18 January 1982

Address to the Bishops of Nigeria at Lagos
15 February 1982

As we explicitly proclaim God's gift of salvation, his call to conversion, his merciful forgiveness and his redemptive love, we do so in the context of the Sacrament of Penance and the Holy Eucharist.

In Nigeria your people have been faithful to the mystery of reconciliation and mercy as evidenced in their practice of going to confession. This fidelity is itself a gift of God. In so many areas in the Church throughout the world, the

Sacrament of Penance, for various reasons, has been used less than before. The Second Vatican Council and its implementation by the Apostolic See aimed at giving renewed emphasis to certain aspects of the sacrament.

These included, for example: the ministry of the Church in the forgiveness of sins; the effect of sin on the whole body of Christ; and the role of the community in the celebration of penance and in the work of reconciliation. But the Second Vatican Council and the Apostolic See in no way willed to initiate a process in which large sectors of the Catholic people would abandon use of the sacrament, or so neglect it in practice as to deny its importance in Christian living. The forthcoming Synod of Bishops will be an excellent opportunity for the magisterium of the Church to reiterate collegially the vital role of this sacrament and its proper use according to the approved norms of the Church. These norms conform to the divine law and express the authentic renewal willed by the Second Vatican Council and the Apostolic See.

Meanwhile, I ask you to do all you can, dear brothers, to emphasize the importance of the ecclesial nature of the Sacrament of Penance, which is not only in harmony with individual confession and absolution, but which actually requires them, except in those very exceptional cases in which the Church authorizes general absolution.

In calling your people to constant conversion, in preaching the mercy and forgiveness of the Saviour, in emphasizing the community aspect of reconciliation and in promoting the proper use of individual confession and absolution among your people, you are rendering a service of immense value not only to your local Churches but to the universal Church as well. You are extolling the mystery of Redemption and defending one of the most sacred rights of your people. As I stated in my first encyclical: "In faithfully observing the centuries-old practice of the Sacrament of Penance - the practice of individual confession with a personal act of sorrow and the intention to amend and make satisfaction - the Church is therefore defending the human soul's individual right: man's right to a more personal encounter with the crucified forgiving Christ.... As is evident, this is

28

also a right on Christ's part with regard to every human
being redeemed by him: his right to meet each one of us
in that key moment in the soul's life constituted by the
moment of conversion and forgiveness" (*Redemptor Hominis,*
20).

O.R. 723   22 February 1982

Address to the Bishops of Eastern France
2 April 1982

For Christians, one of the tests of the moral sense is the
consciousness of sin, the desire for pardon and the process
of doing penance. I recalled this last Sunday at the Angelus:
the Holy Spirit came to convince the world of sin, justice
and judgement; and the Church's mission is to make the
world aware of this, while giving sinners the opportunity
of being forgiven, liberated and made whole again. The next
Synod will be dedicated to this essential process which is
penance, and it is understandable that on the threshold of
Holy Week I should dwell a little on this aspect which
completes that of the formation of conscience and is even
a privileged means of it, while bringing with it the divine
grace of forgiveness. One needs the courage to recognize
one's faults before God, for sins are always offences against
God, even when it is a question of doing wrong to one's
neighbour; one needs the courage to give an account of them
to the Church, which has received the ministry of
forgiveness; and those who have lost a little the sense of
sin and the Church obviously find it hard to accept such a
penitential process. But it is as necessary today as it was
yesterday, and it bears remarkable fruits when it is done
properly. You yourselves are well aware of them. At the
plenary assembly at Lourdes in October 1979, you adopted
a document on "the ministry of penance and
reconciliation". Several French bishops have devoted their

pastoral letter, in whole or in part, to this subject. This week, your priests are going to dedicate, I hope, long periods to this fundamental ministry, which prepares the faithful for Easter Communion. It is of them that I think especially, for I would like to encourage them, along with you, to give a fitting welcome to sinners.

The new rite of penance has highlighted the ecclesial character of misdeeds and forgiveness, and the place of the word of God, which allows one to position oneself better with regard to the Lord's demanding love. It has therefore contributed to a renewal of spiritual life and a new awareness of the values of the sacrament, despite the generally quite de-Christianized environment. And while confessions are presently less numerous, they are undoubtedly more serious and fervent.

But it is also necessary to recognize the existence of a certain crisis in the Sacrament of Penance. Many people no longer see in what way they have sinned, and even less, have possibly sinned seriously; nor, above all, why they should ask forgiveness before a representative of the Church; others give as an excuse that confessions were too tainted with routine and formalism, etc.

There are, besides, serious reasons for astonishment and anxiety when one sees, in certain areas, so many of the faithful receiving the Eucharist when such a small number of them has recourse to the Sacrament of Reconciliation. On this point, good catechesis should lead the faithful to preserve the consciousness of their state of sinfulness and to understand the necessity and sense of a personal process of reconciliation before receiving, with the Eucharist, all its fruits of renewal and unity with Christ and his Church.

The objection is sometimes made that priests, taken up with other tasks and often few in number, are not available for this kind of ministry. Let them remember the example of the saintly Curé d'Ars and so many other pastors who, even in our own day, thanks be to God, practise what has been called ''the asceticism of the confessional''. For we are all at the service of the members of the people of God entrusted to our zeal and, I would say, of each of them.

This feature of individual confession to the priest leads

me to mention certain problems of liturgical and sacramental pastoral care related to communal penitential celebrations. In this area too, when they involve individual absolution, you yourselves have been able to observe some progress made; a catechesis which is well done then leads the faithful to discover the communal sense of their acts, and still more of their state as sinners before God and their brethren, and to give thanks together. This then is a celebration of forgiveness. That is the true grace of this time of Lent: a deepening of the sense of sin which makes us captives and, to the same extent, a pressing desire for liberation and new life with Christ, a life shared in joy, service and brotherly love.

But it is necessary to be careful here: the enthusiasm of the faithful, and especially of young people, for the community aspect of Christian life can incline them to neglect the individual processes which are vitally necessary. This is the case with penitential celebrations when there is general absolution. As you know, recourse may be had to the latter only in exceptional circumstances when it is a matter of physical or moral impossibility and in cases of grave necessity (*cf.* Pastoral Norms for giving General Absolution, no. III). One cannot, therefore, have recourse to it for renewing the ordinary pastoral administration of the Sacrament of Penance. Furthermore, collective absolution does not dispense one from the complete individual confession of faults. This should still take place every time that grave sins have been remitted by a collective absolution (*cf. ibid.* no. VII). The bond between acknowledgement and forgiveness, already inherent in the nature of things, pertains in fact to the essence of the sacrament. I cannot, then, insist enough on the necessity of this personal acknowledgement of grave faults followed by individual absolution which, while being first of all a requirement of a dogmatic order, is also a liberating and formative process, since it allows each person to reorientate in practical terms his or her own life towards God. In fact, a Christian does not exist just as a member of a community: he is an individual person, with his tendencies and his problems, his own background and mind, his temptations

and his falls, his conscience and his responsibility before
God and his brethren. The people of God is not a uniform
flock: each of its members is a unique being in the eyes of
God, and he is so in the eyes of his pastor too, who is, to
each member of the faithful, father, master and judge on
behalf of God.

O.R. 747   16-23 August 1982

Homily: Mass for Young People at Lisbon
14 May 1982

We have spoken about the priesthood, about religious life
and about missionary work as forms of vocation which have
special importance with regard to evangelization, and for
which the Church prays in a special way. She feels called
to this prayer by the Lord's words: "Pray therefore the Lord
of the harvest to send out labourers into his harvest" (Lk
10:2).

But we must understand the words of the Lord Jesus
concerning the "great harvest" and the workers in a more
basic, and at the same time, broader sense than that
indicated in the types of vocations in the Church that we
have just mentioned.

Speaking of the "harvest", of the "great harvest" and
of the "labourers", Christ wishes, first of all, to make his
listeners understand that the "kingdom of God", that is,
salvation, is the great task of all men. Each person must feel
that he is a "labourer", the chief character in his own
salvation: the labourer who is called for the "harvest". Each
person must honestly earn this salvation. And this is also
essential to the entire work of evangelization. "Harvest"
means, therefore, fulfilling the mission of evangelization in
one's self. Each person is called by God's word to this type
of work; especially called is every young boy or girl.

We cannot evangelize others if we are not evangelized

first. We cannot collaborate in the salvation of others if we are not on the path to salvation first.

We began this path to salvation on the day of our Baptism, when, renouncing evil, we chose good in Jesus Christ; we began to live the new life, fruit of his Death and Resurrection. This life must continue to develop. For this reason, he has remained with us in the Church: he has remained especially in the sacraments; he has remained in the Eucharist and in Penance.

Do all of you, my young friends, appreciate these fonts of life? Do you know how to answer the invitation of Jesus - the Bread of Life - conscientiously participating in the Eucharist with the desire to live fully, to conquer evil and to win good? And when it is necessary, because of sin, imperfection or weakness, do you know how to follow the path of conversion and of reconciliation, seeking out the Sacrament of Penance, pardon and life? Form your consciences and be faithful to the Lord, who loves and forgives.

O.R. 740   28 June 1982

Homily at Liverpool Cathedral   30 May 1982

In my apostolic pilgrimage through Britain it is my joy not only to celebrate the Eucharist, but also to administer other sacraments to the faithful of the local Churches. I have already had the opportunity to baptize and confirm and to confer the Sacrament of the Anointing of the Sick. Although it is not possible this evening to celebrate the Sacrament of Penance, nevertheless I wish to emphasize the importance of penance and reconciliation in the life of the Church and in the lives of all her individual members.

Two years ago, the National Pastoral Congress gathered in this Cathedral to begin its work with a service of repentance and reconciliation. Those present prayed for healing and mercy, and for the grace to be faithful to God's will. They asked for light and wisdom to guide their deliberations and to deepen their love for the Church. This evening we assemble around this same altar to give honour and glory to the Lord, to praise our God who is rich in mercy. We see the need for conversion and reconciliation. We too pray for understanding where there has been discord. We seek unity from the same Holy Spirit who grants various gifts to the faithful and different ministries to the Church.

Before the first Pentecost, Jesus said to his disciples: "Receive the Holy Spirit. For those whose sins you forgive, they are forgiven; for those whose sins you retain, they are retained" (Jn 20:23). These words of our Saviour remind us of the fundamental gift of our redemption: the gift of having our sins forgiven and of being reconciled with God. Remission of sin is a completely free and undeserved gift, a newness of life which we could never earn. God grants it to us out of his mercy. As St Paul wrote: "It is all God's work. It was God who reconciled us to himself through Christ and gave us the work of handing on this reconciliation" (2 Cor 5:18).

There is no sin which cannot be forgiven, if we approach the throne of mercy with humble and contrite hearts. No evil is more powerful than the infinite mercy of God. In becoming man, Jesus entered completely into our human experience, even to the point of suffering the final and most cruel effect of the power of sin - death on a Cross. He really became one like us in all things but sin. But evil with all its power did not win. By dying, Christ destroyed our death; by rising, he restored our life; by his wounds we are helped and our sins are forgiven. For this reason, when the Lord appeared to his disciples after the Resurrection, he showed them his hands and his side. He wanted them to see that the victory had been won; to see that he, the Risen Christ, had transformed the marks of sin and death into symbols of hope and life.

By the victory of his Cross, Jesus Christ won for us the forgiveness of our sins and reconciliation with God. And it is these gifts that Christ offers us when he gives the Holy Spirit to the Church, for he said to the Apostles: "Receive

34

the Holy Spirit. For those whose sins you forgive, they are forgiven'' (*Jn 20:23*). Through the power of the Holy Spirit, the Church continues Christ's work of reconciling the world to himself. In every age the Church remains the community of those who have been reconciled with God, the community of those who have received the reconciliation that was willed by God the Father and achieved through the sacrifices of his beloved Son.

The Church is also by her nature always reconciling, handing on to others the gift that she herself has received, the gift of having been forgiven and made one with God. She does this in many ways, but especially through the sacraments, and in particular through Penance. In this consoling sacrament she leads each of the faithful individually to Christ, and through the Church's ministry, Christ himself gives forgiveness, strength and mercy. Through this highly personal sacrament, Christ continues to meet the men and women of our time. He restores wholeness where there was division, he communicates light where darkness reigned, and he gives a hope and joy which the world could never give. Through this sacrament the Church proclaims to the world the infinite riches of God's mercy, that mercy which has broken down barriers which divided us from God and from one another.

On this day of Pentecost, as the Church proclaims the reconciling action of Christ Jesus and the power of his Holy Spirit, I appeal to all the faithful of Britain - and to all the other members of the Church who may hear my voice or read my words: Dearly beloved, let us give greater emphasis to the Sacrament of Penance in our own lives. Let us strive to safeguard what I described in my first Encyclical as Christ's ''right to meet each one of us in that key moment in the soul's life constituted by the moment of conversion and forgiveness'' (*Redemptor Hominis*, 20). And in particular I ask you, my brother priests, to realize how closely and how effectively you can collaborate with the Saviour in the divine work of reconciliation. For lack of time, certain worthy activities may have to be abandoned or postponed, but not the confessional. Always give priority to your specifically priestly role in representing the Good Shepherd in the

Sacrament of Penance. And as you witness and praise the marvellous action of the Holy Spirit in human hearts, you will feel yourselves called to further conversion and to deeper love of Christ and his flock.

O.R. 737   7 June 1982

Address to the Bishops of Kenya

6 December 1982

As pastors of God's people we know the profound need in today's world for mercy. As I mentioned in *Dives in Misericordia:* "The Church must consider it one of her principal duties - at every stage of history and especially in our modern age - to proclaim and to introduce into life the mystery of mercy, supremely revealed in Jesus Christ" (n.14).

In the great event of Redemption, Christ offers to his Church the fullness of mercy, together with loving forgiveness.

The free offer of mercy and forgiveness in a year dedicated to the mystery of Redemption must lead us all to a renewed emphasis on the Sacrament of Penance and on individual confession. It is in the act of individual confession that each person is called to encounter Christ the Redeemer in the key moment of conversion.

By God's grace that moment of conversion is one of mercy and forgiveness and total reconciliation with God and his Church.

And because the Sacrament of Penance is the sacrament of conversion, its use is intimately linked to the fullness of the Gospel message that is proclaimed in the Eucharist: "The Christ who calls to the Eucharistic banquet is always the same Christ who exhorts us to penance and repeats his 'repent'. Without this constant ever-renewed endeavour for conversion, partaking of the Eucharist would lack its full redeeming effectiveness..." (*Redemptor Hominis, 20*).

O.R. 766   3-10 January 1983

Address to Cardinals and Members of the Curia
23 December 1982

It is necessary to rediscover the sense of sin, the loss of which is connected with that more radical and secret loss of the sense of God. The Sacrament of Penance is the sacrament of reconciliation with God, the encounter of the misery of man with the mercy of God, personified in Christ the Redeemer and in the power of the Church. Confession is a practical exercise of faith in the event of Redemption.

The Sacrament of Confession is therefore re-proposed, through the Jubilee, as a testimony of faith in the dynamic sanctity of the Church, which makes saints of sinners. It is re-proposed as a need of the ecclesial community, which is always wounded in its totality by every sin, even if committed individually. It is re-proposed as a purification in view of the Eucharist, a consoling sign of that sacramental economy through which man enters into direct and personal contact with Christ, who died and rose for him: "who loved me and gave himself for me" *(Gal 2: 20)*. In all the sacraments, beginning with Baptism, this interpersonal relationship is established between Christ and man, but it is above all in Penance and in the Eucharist that it is revived throughout the whole span of human life and becomes reality, possession, support, light, joy. *Dilexit me* (He loved me).

O.R. 766   3-10 January 1983

Bull of Indiction of the Jubilee Year
6 January 1983

The extraordinary jubilee celebration of the Redemption is intended, first of all, to revive in the sons and daughters of the Catholic Church the awareness "that their privileged condition is not attributed to their own merits, but to a special grace of Christ. If they fail to respond to that grace in thought, word and deed, not only shall they not be saved, but they shall be more severely judged" (*Lumen Gentium*, 14).

Consequently, every baptized person must, above all, be aware of being called to a particular commitment to penance and renewal, since this is the permanent state of the Church, which "at once holy and always in need of purification, never ceases to do penance and to be renewed" (*ibid.*, 8), as she follows the invitation that Christ addressed to the crowds at the beginning of his ministry: "Repent, and believe in the Gospel" (*Mk 1:15*).

In this specific commitment, the Year that we are about to celebrate follows the same line as the 1975 Holy Year in which my venerable predecessor Paul VI called for renewal in Christ and reconciliation with God. There is no renewal that does not pass through penance and conversion, both as the interior and permanent attitude of the believer and as the practice of virtue that responds to the invitation of the Apostle Paul to "be reconciled with God" (*cf. 2 Cor 5:20*), and also as the means of obtaining God's forgiveness through the Sacrament of Penance.

It is in fact a requirement of one's very condition in the Church that every Catholic should leave nothing undone to remain in the life of grace and should do everything to avoid falling into mortal sin, in order always to be able to share in the Body and Blood of the Lord and thus to be of assistance to the whole Church in one's own personal sanctification and in the ever more sincere commitment to the Lord's service.

Freedom from sin, therefore, is a fruit and a primary requirement of faith in Christ the Redeemer and faith in his Church - Christ who set us free that we might remain free and might share the gift of his sacramental Body for the building up of his ecclesial Body.

At the service of this freedom the Lord Jesus instituted in the Church the Sacrament of Penance, so that those who have committed sin after Baptism may be reconciled with God whom they have offended, and with the Church which they have wounded.

The universal call to conversion fits precisely into this context. Since all are sinners, all need that radical change of spirit, mind and life that the Bible calls *metanoia*-conversion. And this attitude is created and fostered by the word of God - the revelation of the Lord's mercy -, is actuated, above all, by sacramental means, and is manifested in numerous forms of charity and fraternal service.

In order to return to the state of grace, in ordinary circumstances it is not sufficient internally to acknowledge one's guilt and to make external reparation for it. Christ the Redeemer, in founding the Church and making it the universal sacrament of salvation, established that the salvation of the individual should come about within the Church and through the ministry of the Church - that same Church which God also uses in order to communicate the beginning of salvation, which is faith. It is true that the ways of the Lord are inscrutable and that the mystery of encountering God in one's conscience remains unfathomable; but the way that Christ made known to us is through the Church which, by means of the sacrament, or at least the desire for it, re-establishes a new personal contact between the sinner and the Redeemer. This life-giving contact is shown also in the sign of sacramental absolution, whereby Christ who forgives, in the person of his minister, reaches as an individual the person who needs to be forgiven, and enlivens in that person the conviction of faith, on which every other conviction depends: "faith in the Son of God, who has loved me and has given himself for me" (*Gal 2:20*).

Every rediscovered conviction of the merciful love of God and every individual response of repentant love by man is always an ecclesial event. To the power proper to the sacrament, as a sharing in the merits and the infinite satisfying value of the Blood of Christ, our one Redeemer, are added the merits and satisfactions of all those who, sanctified in Christ Jesus and faithful to the call to be holy, offer their joys and prayers, privations and sufferings on behalf of their brothers and sisters in the faith who are most in need of forgiveness, and indeed for the sake of the whlole body of Christ which is the Church.

In consequence, the practice of sacramental confession, in the context of the communion of saints which contributes in different ways to bringing people close to Christ, is an act of faith in the mystery of Redemption and of its realization in the Church. The celebration of sacramental penance is in fact always an act of the Church, whereby she proclaims her faith, gives thanks to God for the liberty with which Christ has set us free, offers her life as a spiritual sacrifice to the praise of the glory of God, while she hastens her steps towards Christ the Lord.

It is a demand of the very mystery of Redemption that the ministry of reconciliation, entrusted by God to the shepherds of the Church, should find its natural accomplishment in the Sacrament of Penance. Those responsible for it are the stewards of the grace deriving from the priesthood of Christ, the priesthood which he shares with his ministers, also in their role as guardians of the penitential discipline. Also responsible for it are the priests, who are able to unite themselves to the intention and charity of Christ, in particular by administering the Sacrament of Penance.

With these considerations I feel closely united to the pastoral concerns of all my brothers in the episcopate. In this regard it is extremely significant that the Synod of Bishops, which will be celebrated in this Jubilee Year of the Redemption, has precisely as its theme Reconciliation and Penance in the Mission of the Church.

Certainly the Fathers of the Synod will, together with me, devote particular attention to the irreplaceable role of the Sacrament of Penance in this saving mission of the Church, and they will make every effort to ensure that nothing is omitted which serves to build up the Body of Christ. Is it not our most ardent shared desire that, in this Year of the Redemption, the number of straying sheep may diminish and that all might return to the Father who awaits them and to Christ the shepherd and guardian of all souls?

O.R. 769   31 January 1983

Letter to the Bishops of the World

25 January 1983

Since one of the main purposes of the Holy Year of the Redemption is to ensure that the renewing power of the Church's sacramental life be lived especially intensely, and indeed, if necessary, to ensure that this power be rediscovered, all of you, dear brothers in the episcopate, will have to make a special effort to present and put into practice an ever more appropriate pastoral strategy regarding the sacraments.

This will include devoting very special attention to the Sacrament of Penance, which is the subject of the coming Synod. This is to encourage a worthy and fruitful preparation of souls for reconciliation with God, through which the grace of the Redemption comes to them personally. The Sacrament of Confession is the irreplaceable means of conversion and spiritual progress. It leads to the restoration of the covenant with God, broken by sin. In the ordinary way it is also linked to the conditions for entering into that means of holiness and forgiveness which we traditionally call by the name of "indulgence".

I therefore repeat, with regard to the pastoral action in dioceses, what has already been said about the need to regain that sense of sin which is so closely linked with regaining the sense of God. Everything that is pastorally effective for evoking in people's hearts sentiments of sorrow for faults committed must be opportunely supported by the means that are available. These include catechesis, frequent penitential services, the presence of priests in the main churches who will ensure that at any hour of the day individuals can receive the Sacrament of Penance.

O.R. 772   21 February 1983

41

Address to Participants in a Congress on "Penance and Reconciliation"

10 February 1983

Your availability to the divine appeal is manifested in realizing, day after day, the compelling word of Jesus: "Turn away from sin and believe in the Good News" *(Mk 1:15)*. This conversion, this change of mentality, is above all the rejection of true evil, sin, which draws us away from God. This conversion is a continuous walk back to the house of the Father, like the return of the prodigal son. This conversion finds its salvific sign in the Sacrament of Penance or Reconciliation. "Freedom from sin", I wrote in the Bull of Indiction of the Jubilee for the 1950th Anniversary of the Redemption, "is... a fruit and primary requirement of faith in Christ the Redeemer and faith in his Church... At the service of this freedom, the Lord Jesus instituted in the Church the Sacrament of Penance, so that those who have committed sin after Baptism may be reconciled with God whom they have offended, and with the Church which they have wounded" *(Aperite Portas, 5)*.

The ministry of reconciliation - this wonderful gift of the infinite mercy of God - is entrusted to you priests. Be ministers who are always worthy, ready, zealous, available, patient, serene, following with faithful diligence the norms established in this matter by ecclesiastical authority. The faithful will thus be able to find in this sacrament an authentic sign and instrument of spiritual rebirth and of gladdening interior freedom.

And all of you, brothers, celebrate the Sacrament of Reconciliation with great confidence in the mercy of God, in full adherence to the ministry and discipline of the Church, with individual confession, as repeatedly recommended by the new Code of Canon Law, for the pardon and peace of the disciples of the Lord, and as the efficacious announcement of the Lord's goodness to everyone.

O.R. 744   7 March 1983

Letter to Priests

Dear brothers, during the Jubilee Year we must become particularly aware of the fact that we are at the service of the reconciliation with God, which was accomplished once and for all in Jesus Christ. We are the servants and ministers of this sacrament, in which the Redemption is made manifest and is accomplished as forgiveness, as the remission of sins.

How eloquent is the fact that Christ, after his Resurrection, once more entered that Upper Room in which on Holy Thursday he had left to the Apostles, together with the Eucharist, the sacrament of the ministerial priesthood, and that he then said to them: "Receive the Holy Spirit; whose sins you shall forgive, they are forgiven them; and whose sins you shall retain, they are retained" (*Jn 20:22f.*).

Just as he had previously given them the power to celebrate the Eucharist, or to renew in a sacramental manner his own paschal Sacrifice, so on this second occasion he gave them the power to forgive sins.

During the Jubilee Year, when you meditate on how your ministerial priesthood has been inscribed in the mystery of Christ's Redemption, you should have this constantly before your eyes! The Jubilee is in fact that special time when the Church, according to a very ancient tradition, renews within the whole community of the people of God an awareness of the Redemption through a singular intensity of the remission and forgiveness of sins: precisely that remission of sins of which we, the priests of the New Covenant, have become, after the Apostles, the legitimate ministers.

As a consequence of the remission of sins in the Sacrament of Penance, all those who, availing themselves of our priestly service, receive this Sacrament, can draw even more fully from the generosity of Christ's Redemption, obtaining the remission of the temporal punishment which, after the remission of sins, still remains to be expiated in the present life or in the next. The Church believes that each and every act of forgiveness comes from the Redemption accomplished by Christ. At the same time, she also believes and hopes that Christ himself accepts the mediation of his Mystical Body in the remission of sins and of temporal punishment. And since, upon the basis of the mystery of the Mystical Body of Christ, which is the Church, there develops, in the context of eternity, the mystery of the communion of saints, in the course of the Jubilee Year the Church looks with special confidence towards that mystery.

The Church wishes to make use, more than ever, of the merits of Mary, of the martyrs and saints, and also of their mediation, in order to make still more present, in all its saving effects and fruits, the Redemption accomplished by Christ. In this way the practice of the Indulgence connected with the Jubilee Year reveals its full evangelical meaning, insofar as the good deriving from Christ's redeeming Sacrifice, through the entire generations of the Church's martyrs and saints, from the beginning up to the present time, once more bears fruit, by the grace of the remission of sins and of the effects of sin, in the souls of people today.

My dear brothers in the priesthood of Christ! During the Jubilee Year may you succeed in being in a special way the teachers of God's truth about forgiveness and remission, as this truth is constantly proclaimed by the Church. Present this truth in all its spiritual richness. Seek the ways to impress it upon the minds and consciences of the men and women of our time. And together with the teaching, may you succeed in being, during this Holy Year, in a particularly willing and generous way, the ministers of the Sacrament of Penance, in which the sons and daughters of the Church gain the remission of their sins. May you find, in the service of the confessional, that irreplaceable manifestation and proof of the ministerial priesthood, the model of which has been left to us by so many holy priests and pastors of souls in the history of the Church, down to our own times. And may the toil of this sacred ministry help you to understand still more how much the ministerial priesthood of each one of us is inscribed in the mystery of Christ's Redemption through the Cross and the Resurrection.

O.R. 788   5 April 1983

Address to a Group of US Bishops

15 April 1983

To proclaim reconciliation means, in a particular way, promoting the Sacrament of Penance. It means stressing the importance of the sacrament as it relates to conversion, to Christian growth, to the very renewal of society that cannot be healed without the forgiveness of sins.

It is our role as bishops to point out that both original sin and personal sin are at the basis of the evils that affect society and that there is a constant conflict between good and evil, between Christ and Satan. It is salutary for our people to realize that they are involved in the continuation of the Paschal conflict - *Mors et vita duello conflixere mirando* (Death with life contended: combat strangely ended!) - but that they are fortified by the strength of the Risen Christ. Only when the faithful recognize sin in their own lives are they ready to understand reconciliation and to open their hearts to penance and personal conversion. Only then are they able to contribute to the renewal of society, since personal conversion is also the only way that leads to the lasting renewal of society. This personal conversion, by divine precept, is intimately linked to the Sacrament of Penance.

Just five years ago this month, Paul VI spoke to the New York bishops during the last *ad limina* visit. With prophetic insistence he emphasized both the importance of conversion and its relationship to the Sacrament of Penance. He stated at that time: ''Conversion constitutes the goal to be achieved by our apostolic ministry: to awaken a consciousness of sin in its perennial and tragic reality, a consciousness of its personal and social dimensions, together with a realization that 'grace has far surpassed sin' *(Rom 5:20)*''. His solicitude for conversion and its various aspects is my own today. His words retain their total relevance for the Church in the United States and throughout the world, and I propose them once again to your pastoral zeal and responsibility.

In particular he requested that priests be encouraged by the bishops to give special priority to the ministry of the Sacrament of Penance. He wrote: ''If priests deeply understand how closely they collaborate, through the Sacrament of Penance, with the Saviour in the work of conversion, they will give themselves with ever greater zeal to this ministry. More confessors will readily be available to the faithful. Other works, for lack of time, may have to be postponed or even abandoned, but not the confessional". Our ministry as priests and bishops certainly means that we are called upon to go in search of those who have sinned, so as to invite them to return to the fullness of the Father's love. In doing so, let us hold up hope and proclaim mercy. Let us, together with our priests, concentrate the attention of the faithful on the person of Jesus Christ the Redeemer, who personally forgives and reconciles each individual. For the glory of the Father let us encourage our people to understand the great truth that "the blood of Jesus his Son cleanses us from all sin" *(1 Jn 1:7)*. Yes, dear brothers, let us emphasize over and over again the immense value of a personal encounter with the God of mercy through individual confession. Let us, with our people, raise a hymn of praise to "the blood of Christ, who through the eternal Spirit offered himself without blemish to God" *(Heb 9:14)*.

In speaking to the group of New York bishops, Paul VI also dealt with the question of general absolution, and its proper application. The experience of the universal Church confirms the need on the part of all bishops for further pastoral vigilance.

The new Code of Canon Law points out again the exceptional character of this practice, repeating that general absolution is not envisioned solely because of large numbers of penitents assembled for a great celebration or pilgrimage: *"ratione solius magni concursus paenitentium, qualis haberi potest in magna aliqua festivitate aut peregrinatione"* (Can. 961, 1,2).

I would ask once again for your zealous pastoral and collegial solicitude to help ensure that these norms, as well as the norms regulating the First Confession of children, are understood and properly applied. The treasures of Christ's love in the Sacrament of Penance are so great that children too must be initiated into them. The patient effort of parents, teachers and priests needed to prepare children for this sacrament are of great value for the whole Church.

In this Holy Year of the Redemption I would ask that a whole pastoral programme be developed around the Sacrament of Penance and be effected by practical means. This will include a renewed effort at catechesis, so that the sacrament can be made a dynamic part of the lives of young and old alike. Frequent penitential celebrations including the individual confession and absolution of sins will be a great help to the faithful in grasping better the realities of sin and grace, and in experiencing the great joy of meeting Christ in an encounter of love, mercy and pardon. The availability of confessors, emphasized and publicized in different ways, such as Church bulletins, can give a great impetus to the faithful to go to confession, since God's grace has already awakened a desire or a need for the sacrament in the hearts of many. Something totally consonant with our priestly and apostolic ministry is for us to invite the faithful repeatedly to reconciliation with God and with the ecclesial community. As pastors, we must be humbly conscious of our weaknesses and our sins, and yet, in God's plan of mercy, we have been given the charism and obligation to call the faithful to repentance and conversion, and to lead the way.

As mentioned in the *Ordo Paenitentiae*, the celebration of the Sacrament of Penance is always permitted during any season or on any day (cf. no. 12). Yet it is particularly appropriate during Lent, so as to prepare the faithful for a fitting celebration of the Paschal Mystery, the grace of which is so effectively presented to them during the liturgy of the Sacred Triduum. The faithful are certainly to be encouraged to confess their sins before these last days of Holy Week as a spiritual preparation for them; at the same time this will help to diminish the heavy pressure on confessors. Nevertheless, I would ask that bishops urge their priests to do everything possible in their pastoral generosity and zeal to make confessions available also during the last days of Holy Week. There will inevitably be people, who, in spite of everything, will need this opportunity of grace. This generous sacrifice on the part of priests will allow them to share even more deeply in the Paschal Mystery and will be amply rewarded by Christ.

As we pursue our ministry of reconciliation let us always look to both aspects of the person's return to God: the reconciling action of God and the response of the individual through penance and conversion. There is no doubt that penance and conversion involve great effort, and are sometimes extremely painful. Thre is no doubt that the word of God is demanding and sometimes the human being is confused in concrete situations which call for much more than human effort and which require humble and persevering prayer. And yet as pastors we must not underestimate the limitless power of God's grace, nor can we attempt to alter the requirements of the Gospel. We are accountable to Christ the Good Shepherd for exercising true pastoral compassion, and we must not be surprised if the world falsely equates fidelity to the eternal word of God with insensitivity to human weakness. On the contrary, the Redemption touches hearts precisely through the revelation of God's word. What we must do is to give the prophetic example of reconciliation, conversion and penance in our own lives, proclaiming by word and example that Jesus Christ is the only Redeemer and Reconciler of humanity.

Let us, dear brothers, walk this path together, united with Mary the Mother of Jesus and united among ourselves and with the worldwide episcopate. In this great bond of collegiality between all the bishops and the Successor of Peter there is great strength for your pastoral initiatives and the important guarantee of their supernatural effectiveness. In the ministry of reconciliation, in the dispensation of the mystery of the Redemption through the Sacrament of Penance, supernatural effectiveness is of supreme importance. Be convinced, dear brothers, that if we walk together, the Lord Jesus will reveal himself to us; he will convert us ever further to his love; he will use us as servant pastors to bring his Redemption to the world.

O.R. 781   25 April 1983

Audience Address 15 June 1983

Dearest brothers and sisters, by sacramentally renewing the redemptive sacrifice, the Eucharist is intended to apply to the men of today the reconciliation achieved once for all by Christ for mankind of every era. The words that the priest pronounces at the moment of the consecration of the wine more directly express this efficacy, insofar as they state that the Blood of Christ, made present on the altar, was shed for the multitude of men "that sins may be forgiven". These are efficacious words: every Eucharistic consecration obtains an effect of remission of sins for the world and thus contributes to the reconciliation of sinful mankind with God. The sacrifice offered in the Eucharist is not, in fact, a mere sacrifice of praise; it is an expiatory or "propitiatory" sacrifice, as the Council of Trent declared (DS 1753), since in it is renewed the Sacrifice of the Cross itself, in which Christ made expiation for everyone and merited the forgiveness of the faults of mankind.

Therefore, those who participate in the Eucharistic Sacrifice receive a special grace of forgiveness and reconciliation. Uniting themselves to the offering of Christ, they can more abundantly receive the fruit of the immolation which he made of himself on the Cross.

Nevertheless, the principal fruit of the Eucharistic Sacrament is not the remission of sins of those who participate in it. For that purpose another sacrament has been expressly instituted by Jesus Christ. After his Resurrection, the Risen Saviour said to his disciples: "Receive the Holy Spirit. If you forgive men's sins, they are forgiven them; if you hold them bound, they are held bound" *(Jn 20:22-23)*. To those to whom he entrusts the priestly ministry he gives the power of forgiving all sins: divine forgiveness will be accorded in the Church by the ministers of the Church. The Eucharist cannot replace this sacrament of forgiveness and reconciliation, which keeps its proper value, while remaining in close connection with the Sacrifice of the Altar.

In the Eucharist there is a special necessity for purity,

49

which Jesus expressly emphasized at the Last Supper. When he began to wash the disciples' feet, he certainly wanted to give them a lesson in humble service, because with that gesture he responded to the dispute that had arisen among them as to who was the greatest *(Lk 22:24)*. But while he enlightened them about the way of humility, inviting them by his example to set out courageously on this way, he further intended to make them understand that, for the Eucharistic meal, there was also a purity of heart necessary which only he, the Saviour, was able to give. He then acknowledged this purity in the Twelve, except for one among them: "You are cleansed, though not all" *(Jn 13:10)*. The one who was preparing to betray him could not participate in the banquet except with hypocritical sentiments. The evangelist tells us that, from the moment that Judas received the morsel given by Christ, "Satan entered his heart" *(Jn 13:27)*. In order to receive into oneself the grace of the Eucharistic food, certain dispositions of soul are required, in the absence of which the meal risks being changed into a betrayal.

St Paul, witness of certain divisions that scandalously showed up during the Eucharistic banquet in Corinth, issued a warning intended for the reflection of not only those faithful, but of many other Christians: "Whoever eats the bread or drinks the cup of the Lord unworthily sins against the body and blood of the Lord.

A man should examine himself first; only then should he eat of the bread and drink of the cup. He who eats and drinks without recognizing the body eats and drinks a judgement of himself"*(1 Cor 11:27-29)*.

Before approaching the Eucharistic table, the Christian is therefore called to examine himself to see if his dispositions permit him to receive Communion worthily. Of course, in a certain sense, no one is worthy to receive as nourishment the Body of Christ, and those who take part in the Eucharist confess, at the moment of Communion, that they are not worthy to receive the Lord into themselves. But the unworthiness of which St Paul speaks means something else: it refers to interior dispositions that are incompatible with the Eucharistic banquet, because they are opposed to welcoming Christ.

To better assure the faithful about the absence of such negative dispositions, the Liturgy provides a penitential preparation at the beginning of the Eucharistic celebration: the participants acknowledge that they are sinners and implore divine forgiveness.

Even if they habitually live in the Lord's friendship, they are aware of their faults and imperfections and of their need for divine mercy. They wish to present themselves at the Eucharist with the greatest purity.

This penitential preparation would therefore be insufficient for those who had a mortal sin on their conscience. Recourse to the Sacrament of Reconciliation is therefore necessary in order to approach Eucharistic Communion worthily.

The Church hopes, nevertheless, that even beyond this case of necessity Christians will have recourse to the sacrament of forgiveness with reasonable frequency in order to foster in themselves ever better dispositions. The penitential preparation at the beginning of every celebration must not therefore render the sacrament of forgiveness useless, but it must rather revive in the participants the awareness of an ever greater need for purity, and with that, have them increasingly feel the value of the grace of the sacrament. The Sacrament of Reconciliation is not reserved only for those who commit serious sins. It was instituted for the remission of all sins, and the grace that flows from it has a special efficacy of purification and support in the effort of amendment and progress. It is an irreplaceable sacrament in Christian life; it cannot be disregarded or neglected if one wants the seed of divine life to mature in the Christian and produce all the desired fruits.

O.R. 789 20 June 1983

Address to Priests at Lourdes

Dear brothers in the priesthood, together, and with the personal and always living remembrance of the bishops who bestowed on us the power to forgive sins, let us join the Lord Jesus himself on Easter evening. According to the account in St John, the disciples were still shut up in the Cenacle for fear of the Jews. And behold their Master appeared to them, showed them his wounds, twice offered them his peace. They were overcome with emotion and joy.

Jesus then gave them a message both simple and solemn: "As the Father has sent me, so I send you" *(Jn 20:21)*. And, with a symbolic gesture which recalls the creating breath in Genesis, he breathed over them a regenerating breath and carefully explained its meaning: "Receive the Holy Spirit. If you forgive men's sins, they are forgiven them; if you hold them bound, they are held bound" *(Jn 20:22-23)*.

O Christ, revive in us and in all the priests of the world this truly paschal gift! This gift destined to make humanity, always inclined to sin, pass from death to life! On that Easter evening, you could already see, Lord, the use we would make of this gift which sprang from your heart, as did the other sacraments. You knew the hours of toil and joy that we would devote to this ministry, so sublime and yet so human. There exist today trends of thought which minimize the notion of sin and, by the same token, depreciate the power of forgiveness given in ordination. Here, Mary had Bernadette transmit the invitation to do penance, and the remarkable momentum of conversions has never ceased. How many men and women have rediscovered, in the chapel of confessions or elsewhere in these sanctuaries, and thanks to our ministry, the peace of a purified heart and the courage to be faithful to the Gospel!

O Jesus, you, the "high priest, holy, innocent, undefiled, ... higher than the heavens" *(Heb 7:26)*, have mercy on those who let themselves be taken in by ill-considered acceptance of dangerous and seductive ideas, also void of realism, which minimize sin and forgiveness! You came into this world to heal and save all men. We give you thanks for having chosen us and having made us like you sacramentally, so that we may continue your mission of reconciling men to God and with each other.

This mission is as much necessary today as it was yesterday! It follows from the primary mission, as recorded by St Matthew: "Go, therefore, and make disciples of all the nations..." *(Mt 28:19)*. Now, to be your disciple, Lord, "is to be clothed with you", as your Apostle Paul often said. According to your teaching and with the entire tradition of your Church, we believe that sin is personal, in the sense that it prevents the growth of your life among our human brothers and wounds your Mystical Body which is the Church.

O Jesus, you whose first apostles confessed your divinity to the point of shedding their blood, we want to admire the way in which they understood perfectly your mission as Liberator from sin which ruins human hearts and minds, even after the grace of baptism. We want to admire their concern for exercising the ministry of penance and reconciliation which they received from you without any possible doubt. The evidence from the early Church is too strong. O Redeemer of the entire man and of all men, convince us always more deeply that you have called and consecrated us for this ministry of reconciliation! You who simply and divinely explained that penance and reconciliation are basically a conversion, a return to the heavenly Father from whom we moved away and a return to our brothers from whom we were separated, renew, especially through prayer, our aptitude and our zeal for this ecclesial service which generates peace and happiness beyond measure.

At the end of this meditation in your presence, we feel very strongly how much you need our voice, our heart, our action, our whole priestly being, to receive in the name of the Church each of our brothers and sisters who desire and even thirst for reconciliation, and to reveal to them the message of your merciful and regenerating love; to each and every one, with his unique history, his particular problems and his special place in the human community which must be restored and whose unity must be knit according to your plan of salvation.

And if, unfortunately, despite our efforts to be available and welcoming, the faithful are too slow in understanding who is waiting for them through the merciful action of the Church, may we understand the meaning of this very trial. We are obviously puzzled by the large number of faithful who abandon this sacrament while only a few turn to it or even return to it in a fruitful way. We will do everything to instruct and convince the faithful of the need to receive forgiveness in a personal, fervent and frequent manner. And we will take great care to exercise this ministry as the Church wants us to, so that no one will abandon it on the pretext that he finds the celebration of the sacrament formal or superficial. But, in reality, neglect in asking forgiveness and even refusal of conversion have always been characteristic of the sinner. Is it not the action of God which reconciles, and forgiveness which changes the heart of the sinner? The priest who experiences sorrow at seeing his brothers abandon the source of pardon, shares in the passion of Christ, in his suffering in the face of obduracy, in his anguish for the salvation of the world. He enters into spiritual combat himself, and he knows that he will need to prepare or prolong his ministry of forgiveness by his own sacrifice, as did the Curé d'Ars. There are devils which can be driven out only by prayers and fasting *(cf. Mk 9:29)*. We knew it from the day of our ordination when the bishop told us: ''Be aware of what you will do, live what you will perform, and conform yourself to the mystery of the Lord's Cross''.

O Mary, Mother of the Redeemer, silently and actively present in this sanctuary of Lourdes as in the entire Church, we turn to you. Grant to all the priests of Jesus Christ the grace of giving to the Sacrament of Reconciliation which Christians so badly need, great importance, much time, theological and spiritual competence, and daily fidelity in the Holy Spirit; because it is the sacrament in which the brethren are reconciled by God, the sacrament which prepares the celebration of the Eucharist, which prepares us to truly live communion in the Church, the Body of Christ!

Beloved brothers in the priesthood, in the name of the Lord I bless the ministry which you will perform here in Lourdes and that which you will perform until the end of your priestly existence.

O.R. 798   22-29 August 1983

Address to a Group of US Bishops

9 September 1983

In every age of the Church there are many meaningful actuations of the priestly ministry. But after the Eucharist, what could be more important than the "ministry of reconciliation" *(2 Cor 5:18)* as exercised in the Sacrament of Penance? What greater human fulfilment is there than touching human hearts through the power of the Holy Spirit and in the name of the merciful and compassionate Redeemer of the world? Like the laity, our priests must strive to serve in many relevant ways every day, but they alone can forgive sins in the name of the Lord Jesus. And connected with the forgiveness of sins is new life and hope and joy for the people of God.

O.R. 802   26 September 1983

Homily in Donaupark, Vienna

11 September 1983

The sign of the Cross forever symbolizes the point from which God goes forth to meet each and every individual who turns to him and mankind preparing for a change of heart. For in the sign of the Cross the love of the Father, the Son and the Holy Spirit has once and for all descended on men. It is a love that never ends. To return to God means to meet this love and to receive it in one's heart. And it means to found one's future conduct on this love.

This is exactly what took place in the heart of the prodigal son when he decided "I will set off and go to my father". At the same time, however, he knew that on his return he would have to admit his guilt: "Father, I have sinned" *(Lk 15:18)*. Penance means reconciliation. But reconciliation presupposes confession of one's sins. Confessing one's sins means testifying to the truth that God is one's Father, a Father who forgives. Those who testify to this truth through their confession will be received by the Father as his sons. The prodigal son knows that only God's fatherly love can forgive his sins.

Dear brothers and sisters, you have centred this *Katholikentag* on the perspective of hope. Consider the parable of the prodigal son, for it is most realistic. In it the perspective of hope is closely linked with the road of return. Consider what such a return involves: an examination of conscience, an active contrition with the firm intention to reform, and confession and satisfaction. Renew your regard for this sacrament, which is the "Sacrament of Reconciliation". It is closely related to the Sacrament of the Eucharist - the Sacrament of Love. Confession delivers us from evil, the Eucharist establishes communion with the Highest Good.

O.R. 801   19 September 1983

Homily: *Opening Mass of the Synod of Bishops*
29 September 1983

When Christ begins his messianic mission, announcing the approaching Kingdom of God - he cries out at the same time: *"metanoeite!"* *(paenitemini!)*, that is, "transform your spirit!". He calls to conversion and reconciliation with God. This calling testifies that turning from evil and directing oneself to good - in its fullness which is God - is possible for man. The human will can receive the saving current of grace, which transforms man's most profound aspirations. In this call of Christ is found the first light of the Good News. It is there opens the perspective of victory of good over evil, of light over sin. It is the perspective that Christ will reconfirm until the end with the Cross and the Resurrection.

Venerated and dear brothers, in the course of the next weeks we must - as pastors of the Church in the last period of the twentieth century - concentrate on this fundamental call of the Gospel. This has been addressed to all men of all times - and therefore also to those of our time. For each it has the saving and liberating power. This power was granted to the Church as the fruit of the Death and Resurrection of Christ. Yet, the same day of the Resurrection, Christ said to the Apostles assembled in the Upper Room in Jerusalem: "Receive the Holy Spirit. If you forgive the sins of any, they are forgiven; if you retain the sins of any, they are retained" *(Jn 20:22-23)*.

As the successors of the Apostles, we have a particular responsibility for the mystery of the reconciliation of man with God, a particular responsibility for the sacrament in which this reconciliation is achieved.

Let us go back again to the reading from the Apocalypse. It announces the victory which is achieved "by the blood of the Lamb" *(Apoc 12:11)*. In this victory "the salvation and the power and the kingdom of our God and the authority of his Christ have come" *(Apoc 12:10)*. In the mystery of the reconciliation with God, in the sacrament in which this reconciliation is completed, man accuses himself confessing his sins - and through this takes the power away from that accuser who day and night accuses each of us, and all humanity, before the Majesty of God three times holy.

In fact, when man accuses himself before God, that confession of guilt, born of repentance, united in the Sacrament of Reconciliation to the Blood of the Lamb, brings victory!

O.R. 803   3 October 1983

Audience Address

The Synod is called to examine the importance of the Redemption in the mission of the Church and to study the ways to better fulfil this mission. Before ascending into heaven, our Lord entrusted to the Apostles and to their successors the task of announcing to all the peoples the Gospel, which is essentially the "good news" of reconciliation with God; of baptizing them for the forgiveness of sins, and of forgiving or retaining sins, in God's name: "Receive the Holy Spirit. If you forgive men's sins, they are forgiven them; if you hold them bound, they are held bound" *(Jn 20:23; cf. Mt. 18:28)*.

The Synod is examining how to understand and apply in the Church the renewing power of the Sacrament of Penance, the gift that gushed forth from the pierced side of the Saviour, the gift that has been for centuries, and still is today, the source of renewal of interior and exterior peace, an instrument of development and growth, a school of sanctity, a training ground for new vocations. From conversion, which is confirmed and strengthened in this sacrament, there springs every true and deep reform of habits, of life and of society; here the foundations are set for a new moral order in the family, in work, in the economic, social and political field. If it is true that "every evil intention springs from man's heart", then it is also true that this heart is capable of listening to the Father's voice, of seeking and obtaining forgiveness, of rising again to new life, of renewing itself and the environment around it.

Let us all therefore ask the Holy Spirit to strengthen the pastors assembled in the Synod and to guide them in their deliberations. Let us pray that the Synod itself, held in this Jubilee Year of the Redemption, will help all consciences to recover the sense of God and the sense of sin, to understand the greatness of God's mercy and the importance of the Sacrament of Penance for the growth of Christians, for the spiritual renewal of the Church, for the moral healing of society.

O.R. 804   10 October 1983

Concluding Address to the Synod of Bishops

29 October 1983

We, in the contemporary Church, must prepare ourselves for the Sacrament of Penance on the basis of an adequately integrated catechesis of penance. Contemporaneously, we must always have before our eyes the profoundly personal character of this sacrament, which does not exclude in any way the social dimension of sin and of penance. We must also keep before our eyes its central position in the entire economy of the work of salvation, its particular link with the Paschal Mystery of Christ and of the Church.

In fact, immediately after his passion and death, on the very day of his Resurrection, on the occasion of the first visit to the Apostles gathered in the Cenacle, Jesus Christ pronounced these words: "Receive the Holy Spirit. If you forgive the sins of any, they are forgiven; if you retain the sins of any, they are retained" (Jn 20:22-23).

The importance of these words and of this event is such that they should be considered alongside the importance of the Eucharist itself.

During the Synod we spoke a great deal about the Sacrament of Penance in the postconciliar period, in the light of the dispositions contained in the *Ordo Paenitentiae*. All these voices were marked by the knowledge that we are dealing with a very deep question. We have no other desire than that of carrying out the will of our Lord, who transmitted and entrusted this sacrament to us in a particular way for the good of the Church and for the salvation of man. This desire was manifested in all the stages of the discussion and is finally expressed in the "proposals" of the Synod.

O.R. 808   7 November 1983

Address to the Bishops of Mexico

2 December 1983

In the recent Synod of Bishops, the Sacrament of Penance was discussed. Indeed, one of the concerns of the Synod Fathers, which is also the appeal of the people of God, is to form all priests - especially those who are now close to receiving the priesthood - with an esteem for the beauty, the urgency and the dignity of this sacrament. We cannot forget that Christ himself conferred on his disciples the ministry of pardon, and that Paul, feeling himself invested with his grace for the apostolate, acknowledges that "God... has reconciled us to himself through Christ and has given us the ministry of reconciliation" *(2 Cor 5:18)*.

Therefore, paving the way for them by your own example, inculcate in your priests the importance of this ministry which Christ and the Church have confided exclusively to the presbyterate for the good of all the faithful. These have the right to receive the grace of the sacrament, so that they can receive light and counsel, direction and encouragement, pardon and grace, when they approach the minister of reconciliation.

In the exercise of this sacred ministry, the priest is identified with Christ the Good Shepherd; he acts *in persona Christi* (in the person of Christ), and by the power of the Holy Spirit he represents the Church which receives the sinner and reconciles him.

This whole sanctifying reality of the sacrament, even though the penitent is its direct object, is also a source of sanctification for the confessor, an exercise of pastoral charity which requires spiritual preparation and a prayerful attitude in the actual discharge of the ministry of confessions to seek light from on high and to foster in the penitent a sense of genuine conversion.

Besides, the members of the people of God know, with a supernatural instinct, how to recognize in their priests Christ himself who receives them and pardons them, and they are heartily grateful for the capacity to welcome then, for the word of light and counsel with which the absolution of their sins is accompanied.

The abuse of general absolutions contrary to the regulations of the Church as clearly stated in the new Code of Canon Law (canons 961-963), is really a violation of the true dignity of the Sacrament of Penance. The faithful exercise of the ministry of the confessions of each Christian highlights the loving attention of Christ for each member of the human race, his personal love for each of the baptized, the capacity to recognize in each one the image of God, and the personal, non-transferable drama for which general counsels and anonymous directions cannot substitute.

Does not the personal and secret sense of sin require as a consequence the same secret and discreet form, the individually adapted and personalized form of individual confession?

In the exercise of the ministry of the confessional, the priest who makes himself readily available for each of the faithful who needs his service, is the visible witness of the dignity of each one of the baptized. The very poorest - as are many of the members of your dioceses - for whom nobody takes time in our restless and hurried society, can give witness - if they are received by the priests with love and respect in the Sacrament of Penance - to the fact that the Church welcomes everyone, that personal love which expresses itself in the care and affection of Christ for each and every one whom he has redeemed by his blood.

O.R. 822   20 February 1984

Address to a Group of US Priests

16 December 1983

St Paul tells us: ''in Christ, God was reconciling the world to himself... and entrusting to us the message of reconciliation'' *(2 Cor 5:19).* As priests, we are charged with being Christ's ambassadors of reconciliation, allowing him to make his saving appeal to the world through us. But in order to fulfil this role effectively, we must first embrace that message ourselves and permit it to take root in our very being. We cannot preach the message of reconciliation to others, unless we are convinced of its saving truth for our own lives.

In your pastoral ministry, there are numerous ways in which you are able to bring the Lord's reconciling love to his people, but perhaps one of the most enriching is found in the celebration of the Sacrament of Penance. Here, in allowing penitents the opportunity personally to confess their sins to the Lord, you mediate one of the most profoundly religious moments of forgiveness and joy. In this sacramental encounter - an experience so deeply intimate - we find Christ forgiving, strengthening and leading each person back to the fullness of life. And he has chosen us, his priests, to be the only ones to forgive sins in his name. This ministry, therefore, is uniquely ours and it is one to which we must give priority.

My brothers, as you return to your respective dioceses, I trust that you will bear witness to this message of reconciliation with new strength and enthusiasm. Encourage your people to have deep confidence in the Lord's merciful love. Offer the needy, the suffering, and those in trouble the comfort of Christ's understanding and consolation. And encourage all to experience the depth of his forgiveness, as well as the hope of his new life which is available in a unique and marvellous way through the Sacrament of Penance. May God sustain you in this work and may he grant to you and your loved ones an abundance of his blessings.

O.R. 815   27 December 1983

Audience Reflection 22 February 1984

Dearest brothers and sisters, today the feast of the Chair of St Peter the Apostle, which we are celebrating during the Year of the Redemption, takes on an altogether special significance. It reminds us of the duty that the Church has in the forgiveness of sins.

The passage from St Matthew's Gospel which we heard contains what is often called the promise of the ministry of Peter and his successors on behalf of the people of God: "I for my part declare to you - Jesus states - you are 'Rock', and on this rock I will build my church, and the jaws of death shall not prevail against it. I will entrust to you the keys of the kingdom of heaven.

Whatever you declare bound on earth shall be bound in heaven; whatever you declare loosed on earth shall be loosed in heaven".

We know that Christ fulfilled this promise after his resurrection, when he ordered Peter, "Feed my lambs; feed my sheep" *(cf. Jn 21:15-17)*. We know also that the Lord Jesus entrusted in a singular way, "with Peter and under Peter" *(Ad Gentes, 38)*, the power to bind and to loose also to the other Apostles and their successors, the bishops *(cf. Mt 18:18)*; and this power is connected in some degree, and through participation, also to priests.

This office includes very vast fields of application, such as the duty to safeguard and proclaim, with "a certain charism of truth" *(Dei Verbum, n.8)*, the word of God; the duty to sanctify, above all through the celebration of the sacraments; the duty to lead the Christian community along the path of fidelity to Christ in the various times and environments.

I must now emphasize the duty of the remission of sins. Often, in the experience of the faithful, the very obligation to present oneself to the minister of forgiveness constitutes a considerable difficulty. "Why - they object - should I reveal to a man like myself my most intimate situations and even my most secret sins?" They further object, "Why can't I address myself directly to God or to Christ, instead of having

63

to go through the mediation of a man in order to obtain forgiveness for my sins?''

These and similar questions are plausible because of the effort that the Sacrament of Penance always requires to some extent. These questions, however, basically evidence a lack of understanding or a lack of acceptance of the mystery of the Church.

True, the man who absolves is a brother who himself also goes to confession because, despite the commitment, to personal sanctification, he is subject to the limitations of human frailty. Nevertheless, the man who absolves is not offering forgiveness of sins in the name of peculiar human gifts of intelligence or psychological insight, or kindness or affability. Neither is he offering forgiveness of sins in the name of his own personal holiness. Hopefully, he is concerned to be ever more welcoming and capable of transmitting the hope that springs from a total belonging to Christ. But when he raises his hand in blessing and pronounces the words of absolution, he acts in the person of Christ: not only as a representative but also and above all as a human instrument in which the Lord Jesus, ''God-with-us'', who died and rose again and lives for our salvation, is present and acting in a mysterious and real way.

It is well to consider that, despite the feeling of discomfort that ecclesial mediation can cause, it is a very human method, so that the God who frees us from our sins does not fade into a far-off abstraction which would in the end become a colourless, irritating and despairing image of ourselves. Through the mediation of the Church's minister, this God makes himself very close to us in the concrete reality of a heart that is indeed pardoned.

In this perspective, we come to ask whether the Church's instrumentality, instead of being contested, should not rather be desired, since it responds to the deepest expectations that are hidden in the human soul when one approaches God and lets himself be saved by him. The minister of the Sacrament of Penance thus appears to us - within the totality of the Church - as a singular expression of the logic of the Incarnation, through which the Word made flesh comes to us and frees us from our sins.

"Whatever you declare bound on earth shall be bound in heaven, and whatever you declare loosed on earth shall be loosed in heaven", Christ says to Peter. The "keys of the kingdom of heaven" are not entrusted to Peter and the Church to be used arbitrarily or to manipulate consciences, but so that consciences can be freed in the full Truth of man, who is Christ, "peace and mercy" *(cf. Gal 6:16)* for everyone

O.R. 823   27 February 1984

Address to Priests and Religious at Bari
26 February 1984

With the universal Church we are living a time of extraordinary grace, which the Jubilee Year of the Redemption is. You find yourselves personally committed. How many times has there resounded from your lips the saying already uttered by the Apostle: "We implore you, in Christ's name: be reconciled to God!" *(2 Cor 5:20)*. And how can you not have felt addressed to yourselves in the first place the urgent call to continual conversion, to interior renewal?

In the Bull of Indiction of the Jubilee Year I wrote that "surely there is no spiritual renewal that does not pass through penance and conversion, both as the interior and permanent attitude of the believer... and also as the means of obtaining God's forgiveness through the Sacrament of Penance" *(Aperite Portas, 4)*.

Permit me, therefore, dear brothers, to call upon you to give ever more value to the Sacrament of Reconciliation. In this, do no more than follow the timely directions of the recent Synod of Bishops. You are in a singular way the beneficiaries and the ministers of the Sacrament of Penance. Who does not see that the priest, constituted by God as the minister of Christ's reconciliation, is called to experience firsthand within himself the gift of reconciliation by making it operative in his own life? We are convinced that it is impossible to offer others the message of reconciliation if we are not capable of living its saving power in ourselves.

In a Church that is called to be renewed, you must lead your brothers and sisters by your example and your life. And by giving the Sacrament of Penance increased value for yourselves personally as a masterly way of purification and growth in the faith, you will gain a deeper appreciation for the immeasurable gift that the Lord has given you in choosing you, his priests, to forgive sins in his name.

O.R. 825   12 March 1984

Audience Reflection   29 February 1984

"We implore you, in Christ's name, be reconciled to God!" *(2 Cor 5:20).* In our common prayer last Wednesday, we reflected on the meaning and the value, even the human value, of forgiveness insofar as it is offered by the Church through the minister of the Sacrament of Penance.

Today, and in the weeks ahead, I would like to continue the consideration of the acts to which we are called when we approach the sacrament of forgiveness. It is a question of very simple actions, very familiar words which, however, contain all the richness of God's presence and require of us the readiness to let ourselves be formed according to Christ's pedagogy, carried out and applied by the motherly wisdom of the Church.

When we believers leave our homes and our everyday lives to go receive the mercy of the Lord, who frees us from our sins in the Sacrament of Reconciliation, what are the convictions and sentiments that we must nourish in our souls?

In the first place, we must be certain that our action is already a "response". At first glance, this emphasis may seem strange. We can ask: is it not we - we alone - who realize the weight of our sins and of the wrongs of our life, who answer for the offense done to God's love, and therefore who make the choice to open ourselves to mercy?

Certainly, our freedom is also required. God does not impose his forgiveness on anyone who refuses to accept it. And yet this freedom has deeper roots and higher goals than we realize. God, who in Christ is the living and supreme mercy, is before us and our plea to be reconciled. He awaits us. We would not budge from our sin if God had not already offered us his forgiveness. "I mean that God - St Paul states - in Christ, was reconciling the world to himself" *(2 Cor 5:19)*. Furthermore, we would not decide to open ourselves to forgiveness if God, through the Holy Spirit, whom Christ gave us, had not already brought about in us sinners the beginning of a change in life which is precisely the desire for and the intention of conversion. "We implore you - St Paul adds - be reconciled to God" *(2 Cor 5:20)*. It is we who appear to take the first steps, but in reality, at the beginning of our reform of life, it is the Lord who enlightens us and makes the offer. It is he whom we follow, it is his initiative with which we comply. Gratitude must fill our heart, even before being freed from our sins through the absolution of the Church.

A second certainty must inspire us when we approach the Sacrament of Penance. We are asked to accept a forgiveness that is not limited to forgetting the past, as though we were spreading a temporary veil over it, but which moves us to a radical change of mind, heart and behaviour, so as to become, through Christ, "the very holiness of God" *(2 Cor 5:21)*. God is a very gentle, but also a very demanding friend. When we encounter him, we can no longer live as though we had not encountered him. We must follow him, not along the ways that we have decided to travel, but along the ways that he has marked out for us. We give him just a piece of our life, and little by little we come to realize that he is asking for all of it.

A religion that is only comforting is a fable, shared by those who have not yet experienced communion with God. This communion indeed offers its very profound satisfactions, but it offers them within an inexhausted commitment to conversion.

In particular - and this is a third aspect of approaching the Sacrament of Reconciliation - the Lord Jesus asks us to be quick in turn to forgive our fellow man if we expect to receive God's forgiveness. The custom in certain Christian traditions to exchange the sign of peace among the faithful before approaching the sacrament of God's mercy puts into practice the Gospel command: "If you forgive the faults of others, your heavenly Father will forgive you yours. If you do not forgive others, neither will your Father forgive you" *(Mt 6:14-15)*.

This emphasis assumes its full importance if we consider that even the most secret and personal sin is always a wound inflicted on the Church *(cf. Lumen Gentium,* n.11), and if we consider that the granting of God's forgiveness, even though this is exclusively an act of the minister of the Sacrament of Penance - the priest - that cannot be delegated, it always takes place within the context of a community that helps and supports and welcomes the sinner back with prayer, in union with the suffering of Christ and with the spirit of the brotherhood that results from the Death and Resurrection of the Lord Jesus *(cf. Lumen Gentium,* n.11).

Therefore, beloved brothers and sisters, let us heed the call of the Apostle Paul as though God himself were exhorting us through him: "Be reconciled to God!"

O.R. 824   5 March 1984

Address to the Provincials of the Capuchins
1 March 1984

You who are called and who are "the friars of the people" and have easier access to the heart of the lowly, can also more easily, especially through the itinerant apostolate, bring Jesus, man's Redeemer, into society, particularly to the large masses of the poor, the lowly, the weak. The people of our times, upset by struggles and wars, by injustices and crises of every kind, need joy and hope, which can be drawn only from the divine Source. Refreshed by it every day, you too go throughout the world, like Francis, saying to everyone: "May the Lord give you peace!" and proclaiming, as "guardians of hope", the salvation which comes from reconciliation with God. The ministry of reconciliation is one of your great tasks, one of your glorious tasks! You must continue in the same glorious tradition. I think that you have the charism of confession, which you must always keep alive in your heart and in your ministry. This great, important charism! Especially in our times when, in human and Christian life, this charism becomes almost a bit abandoned on the one hand, but on the other hand is sought out! During the Synod so many bishops said that if there is a crisis regarding sacramental confession, it is also due to confessors who do not know how to hear confessions well. Now we must reverse this and rediscover love for confessions. And where are we to search for great lovers of confession if not in the Capuchin Order, especially after the canonization of St Leopold?

In this commitment, ever renewed, may Jesus the divine Master guide you, and may the Virgin Mary, who kept and pondered the word of the Lord in her heart, assist you.

O.R. 827   26 March 1984

Audience Reflection   7 March 1984

Continuing the reflection that we have been developing on past Wednesdays, I would like to draw your attention to that particular penance which is connected with the sacrament of forgiveness and which is commonly called "satisfaction". This practice has been rediscovered in its most profound meaning. It even has been made perhaps more significant and more meaningful than it often has been in current usage.

Urged on by God's intervention, the sinner has approached the sacrament of mercy and has received forgiveness for his sins. Before the absolution, however, he has received the assignment of practical penances, which, with the Lord's grace, he will have to perform in his life.

This is not a question of a kind of price with which he could pay for the inestimable gift that God gives us with liberation from sins. The satisfaction is rather the expression of a renewed life which, with a renewed help from God, sets out to be put into practice. Therefore, in its determined expressions, it should not be limited to only the area of prayer, but it should concern the various areas in which sin has devastated man. St Paul speaks to us of "fornication, uncleanness, passion, evil desires, and that lust which is idolatry. These are the sins which provoke God's wrath" *(Col 3:5-6)*.

Furthermore, satisfaction precisely in its connection with and its derivation from the Sacrament of Penance, not only acquires a special efficacy, but it reveals the richness of meanings that mortification has in the perspective of faith. It can never be sufficiently repeated that Christianity is not a gloominess as an end in itself. Christianity is instead a joy and a peace that includes and requires sacrifice.

Original sin, in fact, though remitted by Baptism, normally leaves deep within man a disorder that is overcome, a propensity for sin, which is arrested with human effort, besides being overcome with the Lord's grace *(cf.* Council of Trent, *Decree on Justification,* chap. 10; Denz.-Schön., n. 1535). The very Sacrament of Reconciliation, though offering forgiveness of sins, does not completely remove the difficulty the believer encounters in carrying out the law that is inscribed in man's heart and is perfected by Revelation: this law, even if internalized by the gift of the Holy Spirit, as a rule leaves the possibility of sin and even some inclination to it *(cf. ibid.,* Chap. 11; Denz.-Schön., nos. 1536, 1568-1573). As a result, human and Christian life is always seen as a struggle against evil *(cf. Gaudium et Spes,* nos. 13, 15). So a serious ascetical commitment is required for the faithful to be made ever more capable of loving God and neighbour, in consistent harmony with his state of rebirth in Christ. To this we must add that suffering - that which is undergone with resignation and that which is freely willed with a view to a full conformity to the evangelical counsel - must be lived in union with Christ in order to share in his Passion, Death and Resurrection. In this way the believer can repeat with St Paul: "Even now I find my joy in the suffering I endure for you. In my own flesh I fill up what is lacking in the sufferings of Christ for the sake of his body, the Church" *(Col 1:24)*.

O.R. 825   12 March 1984

Audience Reflection   14 March 1984

"If we confess our sins, he is faithful and just, and will forgive our sins and cleanse us from all unrighteousness" *(1 Jn 1:9)*.

Dearest brothers and sisters, in the light of these words of the Apostle John, we wish, in this meditation, to continue the discovery of the significance underlying the acts we are called upon to perform, according to the dynamics of the sacrament and the Church's pedagogy when we go to confession. Today our attention centres on that moment which Christian asceticism is accustomed to call the examination of conscience in order to recognize our sins.

There is already something demanding in the admission that sin in itself is a decision contrary to the ethical norm which is inscribed in man's very being. It is difficult to recognize in the choice which sets us against God, our true "End" in Christ, the cause of an intolerable separation in the inmost depths of our being between the necessary tendency towards the Absolute and our will to settle for finite goods. Man finds it hard to admit that the evil option disrupts the harmony which should reign between him and his brothers, and between him and the realities of the cosmos.

The difficulty increases out of all proportion when it is a

question not of recognizing sin in its theoretical and general abstractness, but in its reality as an act carried out by a precise person or as a condition in which that definite person finds himself. Then one passes from the understanding of a doctrine to the admission of an experience which concerns us directly and inescapably, since it is the fruit of our responsibility. We are called upon to say, not that "sin exists", but to confess "I have sinned". St John alludes to this difficulty when in his First Letter he warns us: "If we say we have no sin, we deceive ourselves, and the truth is not in us" *(1:8)*.

Perhaps it is necessary to insist that to recognise one's own faults does not mean merely to recall events as bare facts, letting them come back to memory as simple acts of behaviour, as deeds unrelated, as it were, to liberty, and indeed, in some way removed from conscience. The recognition of one's own faults implies rather the bringing to light of the deliberateness which lies behind and within the individual acts which we have performed.

This requires the courage to admit one's own liberty which has been directed to evil. This obliges us to face up to the moral demands which God has inscribed in the depth of our being as imperatives which lead to perfection, when he created us "to his image and likeness" *(cf. Gen 1:26)*, and predestined us to be "conformed to the image of his Son" *(cf. Rom 8:29)*. This requires us, in particular, to "come to ourselves" *(cf. Lk 15:17)* to let the facts speak for themselves: our evil choices do not pass alongside us; they do not pass through us as though they were events which do not involve us. Our evil choices, inasmuch as they are evil, arise within us, solely from us.

God grants us his "concursus" so that we may be able to act; but the negative aspect of our actions depends only on us. It is we who decide our destiny for God or against God, by means of the liberty which God has entrusted to us as a gift and a duty. Still more: when, with difficulty, we come to recognize our sins, we realize also, with still greater difficulty, that we cannot free ourselves from them by ourselves, exclusively by our own power. This is the paradox of human guilt: we can do what is evil but we

72

cannot make amends for the evil committed. We rebel against God whom we cannot then compel to offer us his pardon.

Thus the examination of conscience is revealed to us not only as an effort of psychological introspection, or as an intimate act which is restricted to the boundary of our conscience, abandoned to itself. It is above all a confrontation: a confrontation with the moral law which God has given to us in the moment of creation, which Christ has taken up and perfected in his precept of love (cf. 1 Jn 3:23), and which the Church does not cease to investigate thoroughly and to keep up-to-date with her teaching; a coming face-to-face with the Lord Jesus himself, the Son of God, who willed to assume our human condition to take up the burden of our sins and to conquer them through his Death and Resurrection.

Only in the divine light which is revealed in Christ and which lives in the Church can we clearly detect our faults. Only in the presence of the Lord Jesus who offers his life "for us and for our salvation" shall we succeed in confessing our sins. We shall succeed also because we know that they are already pardoned, if we open ourselves to his mercy. We can let our heart "rebuke us", because we are certain that "God is greater than our hearts" (1 Jn 3:20), and "he knows everything" (ibid.). And for every sin he offers us his benevolence and his grace.

Then there emerges within us also the will of amendment. Pascal would say: "If you knew your sins, you would lose your mind... gradually as you expiate them, you will come to know them, and it will be said to you: 'Behold, your sins are forgiven' " (Pensées 553.)

O.R. 826   20 March 1984

Audience Reflection

''If we acknowledge our sins, he who is just can be trusted to forgive our sins'' *(1 Jn 1:9).* Let us listen once again to the consoling statement of St John.

On past Wednesdays we have been rediscovering the profound significance of the acts that the penitent performs when he approaches and celebrates the Sacrament of Reconciliation, and especially the significance of the encounter with ecclesial mediation, above all in the person of the minister, the significance of approaching and receiving God's forgiveness, and the significance of the examination of conscience and of satisfaction.

Today I would like to reflect with you on an act required for the sacrament which not infrequently creates more of a discomfort to the faithful who are not attentive to the dynamics of the sacrament itself and the true needs of the human heart: I am speaking of the confession of sins. And I insist on *personal* confession - just as I will insist on personal absolution of guilt - since, by Catholic doctrine, individual confession remains the only *ordinary* method of sacramental Penance.

The Church's teaching in this regard is well known. Absolution demands above all, when it is a question of mortal sins, that the priest clearly understand and evaluate the *quality* and the *number* of sins and at the same time the fact that there is sincere sorrow. Why the requirement for such an act?

One could answer with reasons of the psychological and the anthropological order, which would already demonstrate - beyond any superficial analysis - a certain need to tell about himself on the part of the penitent: to tell about himself to someone who will listen with attention and confidence, so that the sinner himself can explain himself and in a certain way feel relieved and freed of the weight of his sins.

But the human perspective does not comprehend the root of conversion, and above all does not give a new life, which is given by the sacrament.

So it is, then, that the confession of sins acquires its truest meaning and its most authentic value in the Sacrament of Penance, where man is called to discover himself fully as a man who has betrayed God and needs mercy.

We must very resolutely state that the confession of sins is not only a moment of alleged psychological self-liberation or human need to reveal oneself in his state of guilt. The confession of sins is principally an act which in some way becomes part of the liturgical and sacramental context of Penance, and shares its characteristics, its dignity, and its efficacy.

The believing sinner, in the heart of the Christian community, presents himself to the minister of reconciliation, who in an altogether special way acts in the name and in the person of the Lord Jesus, and expresses his sins in order to receive forgiveness for them, and thus to be readmitted into the brotherhood of grace.

The judicial connotation that is proper to this relationship is not to be understood according to the categories of the exercise of human justice. The priest confessor must express, in the heart of the Church, the ''justice of God which works through faith in Jesus Christ for all who believe'' *(Rom 3:22):* a justice that is not a condemnation except for those who do not let themselves be saved, but is in itself pardon and mercy.

In the light of this fundamental concept we can understand how the confession of sins is the sinner's clarification of his identity to himself before God who forgives him.

The sinner, in fact, recognizes himself as a stranger and hostile to God through a fundamental choice he has made against God. But this choice is not made as an act of freedom devoid of historical circumstances. It is concretized, rather, in precise acts of behaviour that are precisely the individual sins. Beginning from what he has done, the sinner truly comes to understand who he is:he knows himself as though through induction.

And such a listing of sins is not done in a solipsistic and desperate way: rather it is done by way of religious dialogue, in which are expressed the reasons why God in Christ should not welcome us - here we have the revealing of the sins committed - but with the certainty that he does welcome us and renews us through his favour and through his capacity to re-create us. In this way, the sinner not only knows himself as though through induction, but he knows himself by way of reflection: when he sees himself as God himself sees him in the Lord Jesus; when he accepts himself because God himself in the Lord Jesus accepts him and makes him a "new creation" *(Gal 6:15)*. The divine judgement is revealed for what it is: a freely given pardon.

And so there is cast on the penitent the light of God of which St John speaks in his First Letter: "If we say we have fellowship with him (God), while continuing to walk in darkness, we are liars and do not act in truth... If we acknowledge our sins, he (God) who is just can be trusted to forgive our sins and cleanse us from every wrong" *(1 Jn 1:6-9)*.

O.R. 827   26 March 1984

Audience Reflection   28 March 1984

"If you forgive men's sins, they are forgiven them; if you hold them bound, they are held bound" *(Jn 20:23)*. The risen Jesus passes on to the Apostles the power to forgive in his name.

In the effort to grasp the significance of the acts we are called upon to perform when we approach the Sacrament of Penance, last Wednesday we considered the meaning and the value of the confession of sins as the moment that identifies the sinner to himself before the God of Jesus Christ who forgives. The absolution - the moment that we want to examine today - is, precisely, God's response to the individual who acknowledges and declares his sin, expresses sorrow for it, and disposes himself to the change of life arising from the mercy he has received.

On the part of the priest, in fact, who acts in the heart

of the Church, the absolution expresses the judgement of God on the bad action of man. And the penitent, who is accusing himself before God as guilty, acknowledges the Creator as his Lord and accepts his judgement as the judgement of a Father who does not want the sinner to die but to turn to him and live.

This judgement is manifested in the death and resurrection of Christ: though he knew no sin, "for our sakes God made him to be sin, so that in him we might become the very holiness of God" *(2 Cor 5:21).* The Lord Jesus thus became "our reconciliation" *(cf. Rom 5:11)* and our "peace" *(cf. Eph 2:14).* The Church, therefore, through the priest, in a singular way, does not act as an autonomous reality; she is structurally dependent on the Lord Jesus who founded her, dwells and acts in her, so as to make present in the various times and in the various environments the mystery of the Redemption. The word of the Gospel makes clear this Church's "being sent" in his Apostles on the part of Christ for the remission of sins. "As the Father has sent me, so I send you", says the risen Lord Jesus. And after saying this, breathing on them he adds: "Receive the Holy Spirit; if you forgive men's sins, they are forgiven them;if you hold them bound, they are held bound" *(Jn 20:21-22).* Behind- or within - the human reality of the priest there lies hidden and active the same Lord who has authority to forgive sins and who for this purpose has received and sent his Spirit after the sacrifice of Calvary and the victory of Easter.

We can never sufficiently insist on emphasizing the gratuity of this intervention of God's to ransom us from our misery and our despair. Absolution is certainly not a right that the sinner can claim before God: it is radically a gift for which gratitude must be expressed by one's words and by one's life. And so also: we can never sufficiently insist on emphasizing the concrete and personal character of the pardon offered by the Church to the individual sinner. It is not enough for man in some way or other to refer to a far-off and abstract God. It is a human requirement that coincides with the historic plan carried out by God in Christ and continuing in the Church, the plan of enabling us to meet with a man in the concrete like ourselves, a man who, sustained by the prayers and good works of his brothers and sisters and acting in the person of Christ, assures us of the mercy that is granted us. With regard, then, to the personal character of forgiveness, following the constant tradition of the Church, right from my first encyclical (*Redemptor Hominis*, n.20) and very often afterwards, I have insisted not only on the duty of personal absolution, but also on the right that the individual sinner has to be received and reached in his irreplaceable and unrepeatable originality. Nothing is so personal and inescapable as the responsibility for guilt. And nothing is so personal and inescapable as repentance and the hope and prayer for God's mercy. Every sacrament, for that matter, is not addressed to a generality of people, but to the singularity of a person: "I baptize you (singular)" is said for Baptism; "Receive (singular) the seal of the Holy Spirit" is said for Confirmation; etc. In the same logic we find "I absolve you (singular) from your (singular) sins".

However, it is necessary to be constantly on guard lest a certain individualistic ritualism be followed by an even more harmful ritualism of anonymity. The community dimension of sin and forgiveness neither coincides with nor is necessarily brought about by communal rites. One can have a mind open to catholicity and the universe when confessing individually, and one can have an individualistic attitude when he is lost, as it were, in an indistinct mass.

May today's faithful rediscover the value of the sacrament of forgiveness in order to relive in it the joyful experience of that peace which was the risen Christ's gift to his Church on Easter day.

O.R. 828   2 April 1984

78

"Since we live by the Spirit, let us follow the Spirit's lead"
(Gal 5:25).

Beloved brothers and sisters, during these moments of
prayer on past Wednesdays we have been reflecting on the
Christian and human significance of the various stages on
which the Sacrament of Penance is structured. Today we
want to focus on the fruits, the results, the effects of the
pardon received.

When the Sacrament of Reconciliation finds us in the state
of grave sin and is received with the necessary dispositions,
then it frees us from guilt and restores the life of grace to
us. Certainly the absolution offered us in God's name in
Christ through the mediation of the Church does not remove
the historical fact that the sins had been committed. But by
means of absolution the power of divine mercy brings us
back to that dignity of the children of God that we received
in Baptism.

The catechism has taught us to speak of habitual grace,
that is, a new and divine life that is given to us: this makes
present in us the Spirit of Christ, who conforms us to the
Lord Jesus, so that in restored ecclesial brotherhood we have
to repeat in ourselves the mystery of the Death and
Resurrection of the Redeemer, thus recovering and
revaluing in a new way the authentically human element
of existence.

It is not a question, therefore, of something that is applied
to us from outside. The Holy Spirit returns to dwell in the
believing and pardoned sinner as the Lord Jesus has
promised us; even more, Christ himself, with the Father,
returns to "make his dwelling place" *(cf. Jn 14:23; Rev 3:20)*.

And such a presence is not without happy effects on the
being and acting of the faithful, freed from mortal sin. He
is once more intimately transformed, ontologically changed,
so as to become again a "new creation" *(Gal 6:15)*, a "sharer
in the divine life" *(cf. 2 Pet 1:3-4)*, distinctively marked and
modelled in the image and likeness of the Son of God.

And there is more: the faithful, freed from mortal sin, reacquires a new principle of action which is the same Spirit, so that he becomes capable of an awareness and a new will according to God: he lives by the Father, as Christ, he prays, he loves his brothers and sisters, he hopes for the future inheritance, "letting himself be led by the Spirit", as Paul assures us in his Letter to the Galatians (*cf. 5:18*). And this renewal is not juxtaposed, but it absorbs, heals and transfigures the human element, so that there is need to "rejoice in the Lord" (*cf. Phil 4:4-8*), to "test everything and retain what is good" (*cf. 1 Thess 5:21*).

The Sacrament of Penance, however, is not limited to restoring the grace of Baptism. It offers new appearances of conformation to Christ, which are proper to conversion, insofar as this conversion is ratified and completed by sacramental absolution after sin.

A firm spiritual tradition loves to express this gift that is proper to the Sacrament of Reconciliation in terms of a "spirit of compunction".

What does this mean and what does it imply? The spirit of compunction, basically, is a special union with Christ, the conqueror of sin, passions and temptations. It includes, therefore, a clear and singular awareness of guilt, not as reason for anguish, but rather as reason for joyful gratitude, from the moment that guilt is discovered as pardoned, right up to feeling an almost instinctive disgust for evil. It includes also a special perception of human frailty, which also remains in part even after the reception of the sacrament and can lead anew to "yielding to the cravings of the flesh" (*Gal 5:16*): "lewd conduct, impurity, licentiousness, idolatry, sorcery, hostilities, bickering, jealousy, outbursts of rage, selfish rivalries, dissensions, factions, envy, drunkenness, orgies and the like" (*Gal 5:19-20*), while the restored grace must bear the "fruit of the Spirit" which is "love, joy, peace, patient endurance, kindness, generosity, faith, mildness and chastity" (*Gal 5:22*).

The spirit of compunction, besides, includes the gift of a peculiar clarity in discerning the commitment to the Christian life in all its moral areas and in its application to the individual person, and at the same time it includes the gift of a new capacity to fulfil these responsibilites. All this because God's pardon, received in the Sacrament of Penance, in a most original way creates a likeness to Jesus Christ, who died and rose again to take away the sin of the world and to be "redemption" of the sins of each one of us.

This spirit of compunction, therefore, is not from any sadness or fear, but it is the outburst of a great joy resulting from thepower and mercy of God, who in the Lord Jesus cancels out sins, and to whom we are called to correspond with a delicate conscience and fervent charity.

O.R. 829   9 April 1984

Audience Reflection   11 April 1984

"Let us profess the truth in love and grow to the full maturity of Christ the head" *(Eph 4:15)*

Beloved, in God's plan the Sacrament of Penance constitutes a singularly effective means in that commitment to spiritual growth of which the Apostle Paul has spoken to us. It is by divine disposition an indispensable means - at least in the sincere desire to receive it - for the faithful who, having fallen into grave sin,desire to return to the life of God. The Church, however, through the centuries, interpreting the will of Christ, has always exhorted the faithful to frequent reception of this sacrament, even for the forgiveness of only venial sins.

This development with respect to the past, as my predecessor Pius XII said, did not happen without the assistance of the Holy Spirit *(cf.* Encyclical, *Mystici Corporis).* The Second Vatican Council, then, assures that "the Sacrament of Penance is of greatest advantage to the Christian life" *(Christus Dominus,* 30); and, speaking of priests, it affirms: "To Christ the Saviour and Shepherd, ministers of sacramental grace are intimately united through the fruitful reception of the sacraments, especially the repeated sacramental act of Penance. For this sacrament, prepared for by a daily examination of conscience, greatly fosters the necessary turning of the heart toward the love of the Father of mercies" (*Presbyterorum Ordinis*, 18). And in the Introduction to the new Rite of Penance it says: "Even for venial sins regular and frequent recourse to theSacrament of Penance is very useful. It is not, indeed, a matter of a mere ritual repetition or of a kind of psychological exercise,but rather a constant and renewed commitment to refine the grace of Baptism so that, while we carry about in our bodies the dying of Christ Jesus, his life may be ever more revealed in us *(cf. 2 Cor 4:10)*" (n.7). Thus, for my predecessor Paul VI, "frequent confession remains a privileged source of holiness, peace and joy" (Apostolic Exhortation, *Gaudete in Domino*, 1975).

Certainly, venial sin can be forgiven also in other ways, sacramental and otherwise. Venial sin, in fact, is an act of inordinate attachment to created goods, committed without full awareness or without grave matter, so that friendship with God continues in the person, even if in varying degrees it becomes somewhat marred. Nevertheless, it must not be forgotten that venial sins can inflict dangerous wounds on the sinner.

In the light of these reminders we understand how extremely appropriate it is that these sins be forgiven also through the Sacrament of Penance. The confession of these sins with a view to sacramental forgiveness, in fact, singularly helps us grow aware of our condition as sinners before God in order to make amends; it appeals to us to rediscover in a very personal way the mediating role of the Church, which acts as an instrument of Christ present for our redemption; it offers sacramental grace, that is, an original conformation to the Lord Jesus as the conqueror of sin in all its manifestations, along with a help for the penitent to perceive and have the strength to practice fully the ethical lines of development that God has inscribed upon his heart.

In this way the penitent tends toward "that perfect man who is Christ come to full stature" *(Eph 4:13)*; besides, "professing the truth in love", he is spurred on to "grow to the full maturity of Christ the head" *(Eph 4:15)*.

To these reasons of a theological order I would like to add another one of a pastoral order.

Certainly, spiritual direction (or spiritual counsel, or spiritual dialogue, as some prefer to express it at times) can be carried out even outside the context of the Sacrament of Penance and even by someone who is not endowed with Holy Orders. However, it cannot be denied that this function - insufficient, if it is done only within a group, without a personal relationship - is in fact frequently and happily linked to the Sacrament of Reconciliation and is done by a "teacher" of life *(cf. Eph 4:11)*, by a "spiritual elder" (Rule of St Benedict, chap. 4, 50-51, by a "doctor" (cf. *Summa Theologica, Supplementum*, q.18), by a "guide in the things of God" *(ibid.,* q. 36, a, 1) who is the priest, who is made suitable for special duties "in the Church" by a "singular gift of grace" *(ibid.,* q.35, a. 1).

In this way the penitent overcomes the danger of arbitrariness and is helped to know and to decide his vocation in the light of God.

O.R. 830   16 April 1984

Audience Reflection   18 April 1984

"Let a man examine himself, and so eat of the bread and drink of the cup" *(1 Cor 11:28).* Dear brothers and sisters, we are at the vigil of Holy Thursday, the day on which Christ instituted the ministerial priesthood and the Sacrament of the Eucharist, which is as it were the centre and heart of the Church and repeats the Sacrifice of the Cross so that the Redeemer is offered with us to the Father, he becomes our spiritual food and remains with us in a singular way until the end of time.

Holy Week, which is *par excellence* a time of penance, within and at the summit of Lent, invites us to a reflection about therelationship between the Sacrament of Reconciliation and the Sacrament of the Eucharist.

On the one hand, it can and should be said that the Sacrament of the Eucharist forgives sins. The celebration of

Mass is the key moment of the sacred liturgy which is "the summit towards which the activity of the Church is directed; it is also the fount from which all her power flows" (*Sacrosanctum Concilium*, 10). In this sacramental action the Lord Jesus re-presents his sacrifice of obedience and of self-giving to the Father on our behalf and in unionwith us: "for the remission of our sins" (*cf. Mt 26:28*).

In this sense the Council of Trent speaks of the Eucharist as an "antidote by means of which we are freed from daily faults and preserved from mortal sins" (Decree *De SS. Eucharistia*, ch. 2. Denz-Schön. 1638; cf 1740). Indeed, the same Council of Trent speaks of the Eucharist as a sacrament which procures the remission of grave sins, but by means of the grace and gift of Penance (cf. Decree *De SS. Missae Sacrificio*, ch. 2 Denz - Schön. 1743), which is directed to and includes, at least in intention, sacramental confession. The Eucharist as Sacrifice is not a substitute for nor parallel to the Sacrament of Penance: it is rather the origin from which derive, and the end to which are directed all the other sacraments, and in particular Reconciliation; "it remits even grave crimes and sins" (*ibid.*), especially because it requires and demands sacramental confession.

And here we have the other aspect of Catholic doctrine. As I said in my first encyclical (*Redemptor Hominis*, 20), the Eucharist is "at the centre of the life of the people of God", it requires that there be respected "the full dimension of the divine mystery, the full meaning of this sacramental sign in which Christ, really present, is received, the soul is filled with grace and there is given to us the pledge of future glory".

For this reason the Council of Trent - except in most particular cases in which, in any event, as has been said, contrition should include the desire for the Sacrament of Penance - requires that whoever is conscious of grave sin must not approach Eucharistic Communion without first having received in fact the Sacrament of Reconciliation (Decree *De SS. Eucharistia*, ch. 7, Denz-Schön., nn. 1647; 1661).

Commenting on the words of St Paul: "Let a man examine himself, and so eat of the bread and drink of the cup" (*1

Cor 11:28), I also stated in the same encyclical: "This call by the Apostle indicates at least indirectly the close link between the Eucharist and Penance. Indeed, if the first word of Christ's teaching, the first phrase of the Gospel Good News, was "Repent, and believe in the gospel" *(Mk 1:15)*, the sacrament of the Passion, Cross and Resurrection seems to strengthen and consolidate in an altogether special way this call in our souls. The Eucharist and Penance thus become in a sense two closely connected dimensions of authentic life in accordance with the spirit of the Gospel, of truly Christian life. The Christ who calls to the Eucharistic banquet is always the same Christ who exhorts us to penance and repeats his "Repent". Without this constant, ever renewed endeavour for conversion, partaking of the Eucharist would lack its full redeeming effectiveness and there would be a loss or at least a weakening of the special readiness to offer God the spiritual sacrifice in which our sharing in the priesthood of Christ is expressed in an essential and universal manner" *(Redemptor Hominis, 20)*.

Frequently one hears with pleasure the fact that the faithful today approach the Eucharist with greater frequency. It is to be hoped that such a phenomenon corresponds to a real growth in maturity in faith and charity. There remains, however, the warning of St Paul: "Anyone who eats and drinks without discerning the body eats and drinks judgement upon himself" *(1 Cor 11:29)*. To discern the Body of the Lord means, in the doctrine of the Church, to dispose oneself to receive the Eucharist with a purity of soul which, in the case of grave sin, requires the previous reception of the Sacrament of Penance. Only in this way can our Christian life find in the Sacrifice of the Cross its fullness and succeed in experiencing that perfect joy which Jesus promised to those in communion with him.

O.R. 831   24 April 1984

Address to Confessors

It is truly pleasing to me to meet with you who during the Jubilee Year exercised the ministry of Reconciliation as penitentiaries or as additional confessors in the Patriarchal Basilicas and in other churches in Rome. This offers me the fortunate opportunity to tell you and so many other generous priests who are dedicated to the ministry of confessions some things which I have in my heart.

Above all, I want to thank you for the truly precious work that you did for months and months in the silent, patient, and constant fulfilment of a task situated at the very heart of the Holy Year, because through it - and through you - access to the fountains of divine mercy was offered to innumerable pilgrims. The intention and organization of the Jubilee Year was directed toward this end above and before all, and therefore in a certain sense you have been its principal ministers.

But in you I am pleased to see represented and spiritually present so many other venerable and beloved priests who in the various dioceses of every continent exercised the same ministry during the Holy Year, complying without doubt to the interior impulse of the Spirit, who brought them to respond to the new, more intense, and sometimes unexpected requests of the faithful who wanted to return to this sacramental practice. And my thoughts widen, wishing to include the numerous ranks of our confrères, who, from generation to generation have suceeded one another in the confessionals, in Rome and in all the local Churches in the world, to receive people of all ages and conditions whom the same Spirit drew to the Sacrament of purification and pardon. They make up a magnificent band of bearers of grace, of teachings, advice, understanding, consolation and encouragement toward good, to whom is due, besides the conversion and sanctification of individuals, the formation, safeguarding, and the transmission of that Christian custom which in many nations is the richest and most important patrimony of civilization inspired by the Gospel.

Let us feel united today as participants in this "holy communion" of priests and pastors of souls of all times, associated not only in the bond of ecclesial fraternity, but also in the continuity of a ministry which permits so many humble, good and wise priests to be the artisans of the renewal of consciences, the rejuvenation of the Christian community, the infusion of a spiritual supplement to the same human societies and institutions ever in need of the life-giving breath of the Spirit.

In the ecclesial communion which unites in "one heart and one mind" *(Acts 4:32)*, at whatever time and in whatever place, today I make myself the spokesman for the Church in extending to everyone her approval and praise; I make myself your spokesman in thanking the Lord for all the gifts of mercy and pardon that God has granted by means of so many of his humble servants to innumerable persons always, and especially in the Jubilee Year which ended a short time ago.

We have all been witnesses of what God has done during the Jubilee Celebration of the Redemption; all of us, and perhaps you even more than others, can say with the psalmist that the Lord truly "has done wondrous deeds" *(Ps 97(98):1)*.

These wondrous deeds have had certain external results, especially in the last months of the Jubilee year, as though by need of expansion of the charge of supernatural life accumulated in the souls of the faithful. The young people especially have made explode, one might say, what all the Church had in its heart. But you know that the most marvellous things are those that happened for so many souls at the level of conscience, where human repentance and divine pardon brought them to new life through sacramental grace. This change, this conversion of the soul, through the action of justifying grace, is "the greatest work that God performs in the world", as St Thomas Aquinas explains *(Summa Theologica* I-II, q. 11, a.9), echoing what St Augustine wrote: "It is a greater work that a just man is made from an impious man than to create heaven and earth. For heaven and earth will pass away, but the salvation and justification of the righteous shall remain" (In Joan. tr. 72, PL35, 1823).

87

Indeed St Thomas shows how St Augustine was right by adding: "Let him judge who can, whether it be a greater work to create just angels than to justify impious ones. Surely, if both works are equal in power, the latter is greater in mercy" *(ibid.).*

In Confession, therefore, there is continually renewed and effected, as in Baptism, what we may call the miracle of divine mercy. We cannot allow this fruit of the Holy Year to be wasted. If the Jubilee celebration has confirmed the importance, or rather the vital necessity of the Sacrament of Penance for mankind and for the Church, it has permitted us to ascertain that very many believers are sensitive and docile to the Church's call to this sacrament, because it touches an interior need of theirs, and in many cases a real desire, even if many times unexpressed or perhaps quite smothered by their daily preoccupations and distractions. If there has been victory for the good sower and you, more than any others, have been able to gather such a harvest, it is now necessary to continue to commit yourselves to the ministry of reconciliation with a new pastoral thrust, that is, with a new availability, with new generosity, with a new spirit of sacrifice, and with a new understanding of its function in the economy of salvation as a means of union and a channel of communication between the Heart of Jesus Christ Crucified and individual persons all in need of redemption.

In this meeting with you, dear and venerable penitentiaries and Roman confessors, I want to reiterate this fundamental point of whatever pastoral programme that wishes to conform to the institution and the spirit of Christ and the tradition of the Church.

As the Successor of Peter, the Pope feels the obligation of providing above all and more directly for the Diocese of Rome, where the tradition of the Church has its guidelines also on this point. But I am sure that the bishops of all the world, who are also participants in the apostolic succession, will continue to provide in every possible way that the precious ministry of confession will have the place due to it in the esteem, commitment, time, and in the personal asceticism itself of all priests in care of souls.

In particular I wish to recommend that all parish churches and those of religious orders be assured the presence of priests qualified for the administration of the Sacrament of Penance in convenient places and with more suitable schedules, taking into account the disciplinary and pastoral norms of Canon Law and of particular legislations. Cathedrals and sanctuaries especially assume ever more this function of "places of mercy", where it is always possible to easily find the grace of pardon. Nor should there be omitted the ancient custom of scheduling extraordinary preaching - in the form of missions, exercises, retreats etc., besides the homilies or sermons which are normally given in churches - assuring on such occasions the presence of extraordinary confessors.

The ministry of Penance demands from us priests not only a generous donation of time and work, but also an ardent and sincere zeal for the salvation of souls, which is translated into the practice of the small and great virtues of a good shepherd: for example patience, punctuality, reserve, kindness in manners and word, availability for consultation, magnanimity of mind and heart, and all the other qualities and virtues necessary for the proper performance of this most delicate office.

Only this spiritual wealth frees us from the danger of falling into that lack of delicacy, of goodness, of respect for consciences, of affability, of dedication, which at times can indispose those who approach the sacrament with the hope and confidence of finding there a concrete manifestation of him whom they know as "rich in mercy" *(Eph 2:4)*. We must be his image, his reflection, above all in this! Poor in everything, our wealth can and must be mercy! It will also, and above all in this field, complement justice, which we must also practice; it will attenuate its strictness and sweeten its demands.

In this regard, it will be well to meditate frequently on the fact that we are not the owners of this sacrament nor of consciences: we are instead, and we must take pains to be in an ever more fitting way, humble "servants of the servants of God", "ministers of Christ and administrators of the mysteries of God", as St Paul says. "The first requirement of an administrator is that he prove trustworthy'', the Apostle continues *(1 Cor 4:1-2)*. Faithful to Christ, the Eternal Priest, faithful to the Church, faithful to this sacrament, and faithful to the souls who come to seek from us the generosity of divine mercy!

For this purpose it will always be useful and necessary to possess a pastoral pedagogy, matured in prayer and in experience. This presupposes certain gifts of intuition, of finesse, of kindness, but it is solidified and perfected with the prudent exercise of the ministry and with the charisms granted by the Holy Spirit to those who make themselves his docile instruments: above all the gift of counsel, destined especially to pastors and directors of consciences who, if they are faithful, may come to deserve the title that was attributed to St Antoninus of Florence, *man of counsels.*

Even in our time we have before our eyes marvellous figures of confessors, like St Leopold Mandic, whom I had the joy of canonizing.

In him the Church wanted to honour also so many others, known and unknown, who are found, one could say, in every diocese, in every religious family, and who are points of reference for the faithful and for the priests themselves. How many times, dear brothers, have we been granted the gift to find and receive from one of these venerable men of God the direction which we needed, and which we felt had come from on high!

The confessor must have a light that comes from on high, and therefore a pedagogy of faith that sees and helps others to see everything in that light, that is, in reference to God, the Supreme Legislator, Friend, and Father of infinite mercy, a pedagogy of faith which in that light considers and treats of virtues and sins, and above all draws near to penitents, infusing in them, even in the case of some delicate and fair admonition which needs to be expressed, the sense of the eternal love of God that lives in theheart of the priest.

To no one more than confessors does the exhortation of St Paul to the Colossians apply, which I allow myself to address to you and to all those who exercise this salutary ministry in the whole Church,as a remembrance of this happy meeting and of the entire Holy Year:''Because you are God's chosen ones, holy and beloved, clothe yourselves with heartfelt mercy, with kindness, humility, meekness, and patience.... Forgive as the Lord has forgiven you. Over all these virtues put on love, which binds the rest together and makes them perfect. Christ's peace must reign in your hearts!'' *(Col 3:12-15).*

Faith, love, mercy, peace: these are the spiritual bases indispensable for an apostolate of the Sacrament of Penance which will allow us to confront so many problems and particular cases, but above all to carry out what in the mind of the Church must be the sacred ministry, as it has been, thanks be to God, during the Holy Year and must continue to be, ever more and ever better: an expansion of redeeming grace, which from the Heart of Christ Crucified reaches out to all those who on the highways of life wait and seek the blessed hope of salvation.

With this, full of hope, I bless you from my heart.

O.R. 854   1 October 1984

Apostolic Exhortation, Reconciliatio et Paenitentia   2 December 1984

Among the Sacraments there is one which, though it has often been called the Sacrament of Confession because of the accusation of sins which takes place in it, can more appropriately be considered by antonomasia the Sacrament of Penance, as it is in fact called. And thus it is the Sacrament of conversion and reconciliation. The recent Synod particularly concerned itself with this Sacrament because of its importance with regard to reconciliation.

In all its phases and at all its levels, the Synod considered with the greatest attention that sacramental sign which represents and at the same time accomplishes penance and reconciliation. This Sacrament in itself certainly does not contain all possible ideas of conversion and reconciliation.

From the very beginning, in fact, the Church has recognized and used many and varying forms of penance. Some are liturgical or paraliturgical and include the penitential act in the Mass, services of atonement and pilgrimages; others are of an ascetical character, such as fasting. But of all such acts none is more significant, more divinely efficacious or more lofty and at the same time more easily accessible as a rite than the Sacrament of Penance.

From its preparatory stage, and then in the numerous interventions during the sessions, in the group meetings and in the final *Propositiones*, the Synod took into account the statement frequently made, with varying nuances and emphases, namely: *the Sacrament of Penance is in crisis*. The Synod took note of this crisis. It recommended a no less profound analysis of a theological, historical, psychological, sociological and juridical character of penance in general and of the Sacrament of Penance in particular. In all of this the Synod's intention was to clarify the reasons for the crisis and to open the way to a positive solution, for the good of humanity.

Meanwhile, from the Synod itself the Church has received a clear confirmation of its faith regarding the Sacrament which gives to every Christian and to the whole community of believers the certainty of forgiveness through the power of the redeeming blood of Christ.

It is good to renew and reaffirm this faith at a moment when it might be weakening, losing something of its completeness or entering into an area of shadow and silence, threatened as it is by the negative elements of the above-mentioned crisis. For the Sacrament of Confession is indeed being undermined, on the one hand by the obscuring of the moral and religious conscience, the lessening of a sense of sin, the distortion of the concept of repentance, and the lack of effort to live an authentically Christian life. And on the other hand it is being undermined by the sometimes widespread idea that one can obtain forgiveness directly from God, even in an habitual way, without approaching the Sacrament of Reconciliation. A further negative influence is the routine of a sacramental practice sometimes lacking in fervour and real spontaneity, deriving perhaps from a mistaken and distorted idea of the effects of the Sacrament.

It is therefore appropriate to recall the principal aspects of this great Sacrament.

The Books of the Old and New Testament provide us with the first and fundamental fact concerning the Lord's mercy and forgiveness. In the Psalms and in the preaching of the prophets, the name merciful is perhaps the one most often given to the Lord, in contrast to the persistent cliché whereby the God of the Old Testament is presentedabove all as severe and vengeful. Thus in the Psalms there is a long Sapiential passage drawing from the Exodus tradition, which recalls God's kindly action in the midst of his people. This action, though represented in an anthropomorphic way, is perhaps one of the most eloquent Old Testament proclamations of the divine mercy. Suffice it to quote the verse: ''Yet he, being compassionate, forgave their iniquity, and did not destroy them; he restrained his anger often, and did not stir up all his wrath. He remembered that they were but flesh, a wind that passes and comes not again'' (Ps 78(77):38f.)

In the fullness of time, the Son of God, coming as the Lamb who takes away and bears upon himself the sin of the world, appears as the one who has the power both to judge and to forgive sins, and who has come not to condemn but to forgive and save.

Now this power to forgive sins Jesus confers, through the Holy Spirit, upon ordinary men, themselves subject to the snare of sin, namely his Apostles: ''Receive, the Holy Spirit. Whose sins you shall forgive, they are forgiven; whose sins you shall retain, they are retained'' (Jn 20:22). This is one of the most awe-inspiring innovations of the Gospel! He confers this power on the Apostles also as something which they can transmit - as the Church has understood it from the beginning - to their successors, charged by the same Apostles with the mission and responsibility of continuing their work as proclaimers of the Gospel and ministers of Christ's redemptive work.

Here there is seen in all its grandeur the figure of the minister of the Sacrament of Penance, who by very ancient custom is called the Confessor.

Just as at the altar where he celebrates the Eucharist and just as in each one of the Sacraments, so the priest, as the minister of Penance, acts "*in persona Christi*". The Christ whom he makes present and who accomplishes the mystery of the forgiveness of sins is the Christ who appears as the brother of man, the merciful High Priest, faithful and compassionate, the Shepherd intent on finding the lost sheep, the Physician who heals and comforts, the one Master who teaches the truth and reveals the ways of God, the Judge of the living and the dead, who judges according to the truth and not according to appearances.

This is undoubtedly the most difficult and sensitive, the most exhausting and demanding ministry of the priest, but also one of the most beautiful and consoling. Precisely for this reason and with awareness also of the strong recommendation of the Synod, I will never grow weary of exhorting my brothers, the bishops and priests, to the faithful and diligent performance of this ministry. Before the consciences of the faithful, who open up to him with a mixture of fear and trust, the confessor is called to a lofty task which is one of service to penance and human reconciliation. It is a task of learning the weaknesses and falls of those faithful people, assessing their desire for renewal and their efforts to achieve it, discerning the action of the Holy Spirit in their hearts, imparting to them a forgiveness which God alone can grant, celebrating their reconciliation with the Father, portrayed in the parable of the Prodigal Son, reinstating these redeemed sinners in the ecclesial community with their brothers and sisters, and paternally admonishing these penitents with a firm, encouraging and friendly "Do not sin again" (*Jn 8:11*).

For the effective performance of this ministry, the confessor must necessarily have human qualities of prudence, discretion, discernment and a firmness tempered by gentleness and kindness. He must likewise have a serious and careful preparation, not fragmentary but complete and harmonious, in the different branches of theology, pedagogy and psychology, in the methodology of dialogue, and above all in a living and communicable knowledge of the word of God. But it is even more necessary that he should live an intense and genuine spiritual life. In order to lead others along the path of Christian perfection the minister of Penance himself must first travel this path. More by actions than by long speeches he must give proof of real experience of lived prayer, the practice of the theological and moral virtues of the Gospel, faithful obedience to the will of God, love of the Church and docility to her magisterium.

All this fund of human gifts, Christian virtues and pastoral capabilities has to be worked for and is only acquired with effort.

Every priest must be trained for the ministry of sacramental Penance from his years in the seminary, not only through the study of dogmatic, moral, spiritual and pastoral theology (which are simply parts of a whole), but also through the study of the human sciences, training in dialogue and especially in how to deal with people in the pastoral context. He must then be guided and looked after in his first activities. He must always ensure his own improvement and updating by means of permanent study. What a wealth of grace, true life and spiritual radiation would be poured out on the Church if every priest were careful never to miss, through negligence or various excuses, the appointment with the faithful in the confessional, and if he were even more careful never to go to it unprepared or lacking the necessary human qualities and spiritual and pastoral preparation!

In this regard I cannot but recall with devout admiration those extraordinary apostles of the confessional such as St John Nepomucene, St John Vianney, St Joseph Cafasso and St Leopold of Castelnuovo, to mention only the best known confessors whom the Church has added to the list of her saints. But I also wish to pay homage to the innumerable host of holy and almost always anonymous confessors to whom is owed the salvation of so many souls who have been helped by them in conversion, in the struggle against sin and temptation, in spiritual progress and, in a word, in achieving holiness. I do not hesitate to say that even the great canonized saints are generally the fruit of those confessionals, and not only the saints but also the spiritual patrimony of the Church and the flowering of a civilization permeated with the Christian spirit! Praise then to this silent army of our brothers who have served well and serve each day the cause of reconciliation through the ministry of sacramental Penance!

From the revelation of the value of this ministry and power to forgive sins, conferred by Christ on the Apostles and their successors, there developed in the Church an awareness of the sign of forgiveness, conferred through the Sacrament of Penance. It is the certainty that the Lord Jesus himself instituted and entrusted to the Church - as a gift of his goodness and loving kindness to be offered to all - a special Sacrament for the forgiveness of sins committed after Baptism.

The practice of this Sacrament, as regards its celebration and form, has undergone a long process of development, as is attested to by the most ancient sacramentaries, the documents of Councils and Episcopal Synods, the preaching of the Fathers and the teachingof the Doctors of the Church. But with regard to the substance of the Sacrament there has always remained firm and unchanged in the consciousness of the Church the certainty that, by the will of Christ, forgiveness is offered to each individual by means of sacramental absolution given by the ministers of Penance. It is a certainty reaffirmed with particular vigour both by the Council of Trent and by the Second Vatican Council: "Those who approach the Sacrament of Penance obtain pardon from God's mercy for the offences committed against him, and are, at the same time, reconciled with the Church which they have wounded by their sins and which by charity, by example and by prayer works for their conversion" (*Lumen Gentium*, 11). And as an essential element of faith concerning the value and purpose of Penance it must be reaffirmed that our Saviour Jesus Christ instituted in his Church the Sacrament of Penance so that the faithful who have fallen into sin after Baptism might receive grace and be reconciled with God.

The Church's faith in this Sacrament involves certain other fundamental truths which cannot be disregarded. The sacramental rite of Penance, in its evolution and variation of actual forms, has always preserved and highlighted these truths. When it recommended a reform of this rite, the Second Vatican Council intended to ensure that it would express those truths even more clearly, and this has come about with the new Rite of Penance. For the latter has made its own the whole of the teaching brought together by the Council of Trent, transferring it from its particular historical context (that of a resolute effort to clarify doctrine in the face of the serious deviations from the Church's genuine teaching), in order to translate it faithfully into terms more in keeping with the context of our own time.

The truths mentioned above, powerfully and clearly confirmed by the Synod and contained in the *Propositiones*, can be summarized in the following convictions of faith, to which are connected all the other affirmations of the Catholic doctrine on the Sacrament of Penance.

The first conviction is that, for a Christian, the Sacrament of Penance is the ordinary way of obtaining forgiveness and the remission of serious sins committed after Baptism. Certainly, the Saviour and his salvific action are not so bound to a sacramental sign as to be unable in any period or area of the history of salvation to work outside and above the Sacraments. But in the school of faith we learn that the same Saviour desired and provided that the simple and precious Sacraments of faith would ordinarily be the effective means through which his redemptive power passes and operates. It would therefore be foolish, as well as presumptuous, to wish arbitrarily to disregard the means of grace and salvation which the Lord has provided and, in the specific case, to claim to receive forgiveness while doing without the Sacrament which was instituted by Christ precisely for forgiveness. The renewal of the rites carried out after the Council does not sanction any illusion or alteration in this direction. According to the Church's intention, it was and is meant to stir up in each one of us a new impulse towards the renewal of our interior attitude; towards a deeper understanding of the nature of the Sacrament of Penance; towards a reception of the Sacrament which is more filled with faith, not anxious but trusting; towards a more frequent celebration of the Sacrament which is seen to be completely filled with the Lord's merciful love.

The second conviction concerns the function of the Sacrament of Penance for those who have recourse to it. According to the most ancient traditional idea, the Sacrament is a kind of judicial action; but this takes place before a tribunal of mercy rather than of strict and rigorous justice, which is comparable to human tribunals only by analogy, namely insofar as sinners reveal their sins and their condition as creatures subject to sin; they commit themselves to renouncing and combatting sin; accept the punishment (sacramental penance) which the confessor imposes on them and receive absolution from him.

But as it reflects on the function of this Sacrament, the Church's consciousness discerns in it, over and above the character of judgement in the sense just mentioned, a healing of a medicinal character. And this is linked to the fact that the Gospel frequently presents Christ as healer, while his redemptive work is often called, from Christian antiquity, *"medicina salutis"*. "I wish to heal, not accuse", St Augustine said, referring to the exercise of the pastoral activity regarding Penance (*Sermo* 82, 8: PL38, 511), and it is thanks to the medicine of Confession that the experience of sin does not degenerate into despair. The Rite of Penance alludes to this healing aspect of the Sacrament (*Ordo Paenitentiae*, 6c), to which modern man is perhaps more sensitive, seeing as he does in sin the elementof error but even more the element of weakness and human frailty.

Whether as a tribunal of mercy or a place of spiritual healing, under both aspects the Sacrament requires a knowledge of the sinner's heart, in order to be able to judge and absolve, to cure and heal. Precisely for this reason the Sacrament involves, on the part of the penitent, a sincere and complete confession of sins. This therefore has a *raison d'être* not only inspired by ascetical purposes (as an exercise of humility and mortification) but one that is inherent in the very nature of the Sacrament.

The third conviction, which is one that I wish to emphasize,concerns the realities or parts which make up the sacramental sign of forgiveness and reconciliation. Some of these realities are acts of the penitent, of varying importance but each indispensable either for the validity, the completeness or the fruitfulness of the sign.

First of all, an indispensable condition is the rectitude and clarity of the penitent's conscience. People cannot come to true and genuine repentance until they realize that sin is contrary to the ethical norm written in their inmost being; until they admit that sin has introduced a division into their consciences, which then pervades their whole being and separates them from God and from their brothers and sisters. The sacramental sign of this clarity of conscience is the act traditionally called the examination of conscience, an act that must never be one of anxious psychological introspection but a sincere and calm comparison with the interiormoral law, with the evangelical norms proposed by the Church, with Jesus Christ himself who is our Teacher and Model of life, and with the heavenly Father, who calls us to goodness and perfection.

But the essential act of penance, on the part of the penitent, is contrition, a clear and decisive rejection of the sin committed, together with a resolution not to commit it again, out of love which one has for God and which is reborn with repentance. Understood in this way contrition is therefore the beginning and the heart of conversion, of that evangelical *metanoia* which brings the person back to God like the Prodigal Son returning to his father, and which has in the Sacrament of Penance its visible sign and which perfects attrition. Hence "upon this contrition of heart depends the truth of penance" (*Ordo Paenitentiae*, 6 c).

While reiterating everything that the Church, inspired by God's word, teaches about contrition, I particularly wish to emphasize here just one aspect of this doctrine. It is one that should be better known and considered. Conversion and contrition are often considered under the aspect of the undeniable demands which they involve and under the aspect of the mortification which they impose for the purpose of bringing about a radical change of life. But we do well to recall and emphasize the fact that contrition and conversion are even more a drawing near to the holiness of God, a rediscovery of one's true identity which has been upset and disturbed by sin, a liberation in the very depth of self and thus a regaining of lost joy, the joy of being saved, which the majority of people in our time are no longer capable of experiencing.

We therefore understand why, from the earliest Christian times, in line with the Apostles and with Christ, the Church has included in the sacramental sign of penance the confession of sins. This latter takes on such importance that for centuries the usual name of the Sacrament has been and still is that of Confession. The confession of sins is required, first of all, because the sinner must be known by the person who in the Sacrament exercises the role of judge. He has to evaluate both the seriousness of the sins and repentance of the penitent; he also exercises the role of healer, and must acquaint himself with the condition of the sick person in order to treat and heal him. But the individual confession also has the value of a sign: a sign of the meeting of the sinner with the mediation of the Church in the person of the minister; a sign of the person's revealing of self as a sinner in the sight of God and the Church, of facing his own sinful condition in the eyes of God. The confession of sins therefore cannot be reduced to a mere attempt at psychological self-liberation, even though it corresponds to that legitimate and natural need, inherent in the human heart, to open oneself to another. It is a liturgical act, solemn in its dramatic nature, yet humble and sober in the grandeur of its meaning. It is the act of the Prodigal Son who returns to his Father and is welcomed by him with the kiss of peace. It is an act of honesty and courage. It is an act of entrusting oneself, beyond sin, to the mercy that forgives. Thus we understand why the confession of sins must ordinarily be individual and not collective, just as sin is a deeply personal matter. But at the same time this confession in a way forces sin out of the secret of the heart and thus out of the area of pure individuality, emphasizing its social character as well, for through the minister of Penance it is the ecclesial community, which has been wounded by sin, that welcomes anew the repentant and forgiven sinner.

The other essential stage of the Sacrament of Penance this time belongs to the confessor as judge and healer, a figure of God the Father welcoming and forgiving the one who returns: this is the absolution. The words which express it and the gestures that accompany it in the old and in the new Rite of Penance are significantly simple in their grandeur.

The sacramental formula "I absolve you..." and the imposition of the hand and the sign of the Cross made over the penitent show that at this moment the contrite and converted sinner comes into contact with the power and mercy of God. It is the moment at which, in response to the penitent, the Trinity becomes present in order to blot out sin and restore innocence. And the saving power of the Passion, Death and Resurrection of Jesus is also imparted to the penitent as the "mercy stronger than sin and offence", as I defined it in my Encyclical *Dives in Misericordia*. God is always the one who is principally offended by sin - "against you alone have I sinned!" - and God alone can forgive. Hence the absolution that the priest, the minister of forgiveness, though himself a sinner, grants to the penitent, is the effective sign of the intervention of the Father in every absolution and the sign of the resurrection from spiritual death which is renewed each time that the Sacrament of Penance is administered. Only faith can give us certainty that at that moment every sin is forgiven and blotted out by the mysterious intervention of the Saviour.

Satisfaction is the final act which crowns the sacramental sign of Penance. In some countries the act which the forgiven and absolved penitent agrees to perform after receiving absolution is called precisely the penance. What is the meaning of this satisfaction that one makes or the penance that one performs? Certainly it is not a price that one pays for the sin absolved and for the forgiveness obtained: no human price can match what is obtained, which is the fruit of Christ's Precious Blood. Acts of satisfaction - which, while remaining simple and humble, should be made to express more clearly all that they signify - mean a number of valuable things: They are the sign of the personal commitment that the Christian has made to God, in the Sacrament, to begin a new life (and therefore they should not be reduced to mere formulas to be recited, but should consist of acts of worship, charity, mercy or reparation). They include the idea that the pardoned sinner is able to join his own physical and spiritual mortification - which has been sought after or at least accepted - to the Passion of Jesus who has obtained the forgiveness for him.

They remind us that even after absolution there remains in the Christian a dark area, due to the wound of sin, to the imperfection of love in repentance, to the weakening of the spiritual faculties. It is an area in which there still operates an infectious source of sin which must always be fought with mortification and penance. This is the meaning of the humble but sincere act of satisfaction.

There remains to be made a brief mention of other important convictions about the Sacrament of Penance.

First of all, it must be emphasized that nothing is more personal and intimate than this Sacrament, in which the sinner stands alone before God with his sin, repentance and trust. No one can repent in his place or ask forgiveness in his name. There is a certain solitude of the sinner in his sin and this can be seen dramatically represented in Cain with sin "crouching at his door", as the Book of Genesis says so effectively, and with the distinctive mark on his forehead; in David, admonished by the prophet Nathan; or in the Prodigal Son when he realizes the condition to which he has reduced himself by staying away from his father and decides to return to him. Everything takes place between the individual alone and God. But at the same time one cannot deny the social nature of this Sacrament, in which the whole Church - militant, suffering and glorious in heaven - comes to the aid of the penitent and welcomes him again into her bosom, especially as it was the whole Church which had been offended and wounded by his sin. As the minister of Penance, the priest, by virtue of his sacred office, appears as the witness and representative of this ecclesial nature of the Sacrament. The individual nature and ecclesial nature are two complementary aspects of the Sacrament which the progressive reform of the Rite of Penance, especially that contained in the *Ordo Paenitentiae* promulgated by Paul VI, has sought to emphasize and to make more meaningful in its celebration.

Secondly, it must be emphasized that the most precious result of the forgiveness obtained in the Sacrament of Penance consists in reconciliation with God, which takes place in the inmost heart of the son who was lost and found again, which every penitent is. But it has to be added that this reconciliation with God leads, as it were, to other reconciliations, which repair the breaches caused by sin. The forgiven penitent is reconciled with himself in his inmost being, where he regains his own true identity. He is reconciled with his brethren whom he has in some way attacked and wounded. He is reconciled with the Church. He is reconciled with all creation.

As a result of an awareness of this, at the end of the celebration there arises in the penitent a sense of gratitude to God for the gift of divine mercy received, and the Church invites the penitent to have this sense of gratitude.

Every confessional is a special and blessed place from which, with divisions wiped away, there is born new and uncontaminated a reconciled individual - a reconciled world!

Lastly, I particularly wish to speak of one final consideration, one which concerns all of us priests, who are the ministers of the Sacrament of Penance. The priest's celebration of the Eucharist and administration of the other Sacraments, his pastoral zeal, his relationship with the faithful, his communion with his brother priests, his collaboration with his bishop, his life of prayer - in a word, the whole of his priestly existence, suffers an inexorable decline if by negligence or for some other reason he fails to receive the Sacrament of Penance at regular intervals and in a spirit of genuine faith and devotion. If a priest were no longer to go to confession or properly confess his sins, his priestly being and his priestly action would feel its effects very soon, and this would also be noticed by the community of which he was the pastor.

But I also add that even in order to be a good and effective minister of Penance the priest needs to have recourse to the source of grace and holiness present in this Sacrament. We priests, on the basis of our personal experience, can certainly say that, the more careful we are to receive the Sacrament of Penance and to approach it frequently and with good dispositions, the better we fulfil our own ministry as confessors and ensure that our penitents benefit from it. And on the other hand this ministry would lose much of its effectiveness if in some way we were to stop being good penitents. Such is the integral logic of this great Sacrament.

It invites all of us priests of Christ to pay renewed attention to our personal confession.

Personal experience in its turn becomes and must become today an incentive for the diligent, regular, patient and fervent exercise of the sacred ministry of Penance, to which we are committed by the very fact of our priesthood and our vocation as pastors and servants of our brothers and sisters. Also with this present Exhortation I therefore address an earnest invitation to all the priests of the world, especially to my brothers in the episcopacy and to pastors of souls, an invitation to make every effort to encourage the faithful to make use of this Sacrament. I urge them to use all possible and suitable means to ensure that the greatest possible number of our brothers and sisters receive the grace that has been given to us through Penance for the reconciliation of every soul and of the whole world with God in Christ.

Following the suggestions of the Second Vatican Council, the *Ordo Paenitentiae* provided three rites which, while always keeping intact the essential elements, make it possible to adapt the celebration of the Sacrament of Penance to particular pastoral circumstances.

The first form - reconciliation of individual penitents - is the only normal and ordinary way of celebrating the Sacrament, and it cannot and must not be allowed to fall into disuse or to be neglected. The second form - reconciliation of a number of penitents with individual confession and absolution - even though in the preparatory acts it helps to give greater emphasis to the community aspects of the Sacrament, is the same as the first form in the culminating sacramental act, namely, individual confession and individual absolution of sins. It can thus be regarded as equal to the first form as regards the normality of the rite. The third form however - reconciliation of a number of penitents with general confession and absolution - is exceptional in character. It is therefore not left to free choice but is regulated by a special discipline.

The first form makes possible a highlighting of the more personal - and essential - aspects which are included in the penitential process. The dialogue between penitent and confessor, the sum of the elements used (the biblical texts, the choice of the forms of satisfaction, etc.) make the sacramental celebration correspond more closely to the concrete situation of the penitent. The value of these elements is perceived when one considers the different reasons that bring a Christian to sacramental Penance: a need for personal reconciliation and readmission to friendship with God by regaining the grace lost by sin; a need to check one's spiritual progress and sometimes a need for a more accurate discernment of one's vocation; on many other occasions a need and a desire to escape from a state of spiritual apathy and religious crisis. Thanks then to its individual character, the first form of celebration makes it possible to link the Sacrament of Penance with something which is different but readily linked with it: I am referring to spiritual direction. So it is certainly true that personal decision and commitment are clearly signified and promoted in this first form.

The second form of celebration, precisely by its specific dimension, highlights certain aspects of great importance: the word of God listened to in common has a remarkable effect as compared to its individual reading, and better emphasizes the ecclesial character of conversion and reconciliation. It is particularly meaningful at various seasons of the liturgical year and in connection with events of special pastoral importance. The only point that needs mentioning here is that for celebrating the second form there should be an adequate number of confessors present.

It is therefore natural that the criteria for deciding which of the two forms of celebration to use should be dictated not by situational and subjective reasons but by a desire to secure the true spiritual good of the faithful, in obedience to the penitential discipline of the Church.

We shall also do well to recall that, for a balanced spiritual and pastoral orientation in this regard, great importance must continue to be given to teaching the faithful also to make use of the Sacrament of Penance for venial sins alone, as is borne out by a centuries-old doctrinal tradition and practice.

Though the Church knows and teaches that venial sins

are forgiven in other ways too - for instance, by acts of sorrow, works of charity, prayer, penitential rites - she does not cease to remind everyone of the special usefulness of the sacramental moment for these sins too. The frequent use of the Sacrament - to which some categories of the faithful are in fact held - strengthens the awareness that even minor sins offend God and harm the Church, the Body of Christ. Its celebration then becomes for the faithful "the occasion and the incentive to conform themselves more closely to Christ and to make themselves more docile to the voice of the Spirit" (*Ordo Paenitentiae*, 7 c). Above all it should be emphasized that the grace proper to the sacramental celebration has a great remedial power and helps to remove the very roots of sin.

Attention to the actual celebration, with special reference to the importance of the word of God which is read, recalled and explained, when this is possible and suitable, to the faithful and with them, will help to give fresh life to the practice of the Sacrament and prevent it from declining into a mere formality and routine. The penitent will be helped rather to discover that he or she is living a salvific event, capable of inspiring fresh life and giving true peace of heart. This careful attention to the celebration will also lead the individual Churches to arrange special times for the celebration of the Sacrament. It will also be an incentive to teaching the faithful, especially children and young people, to accustom themselves to keeping to these times, except in cases of necessity, when the parish priest must always show a ready willingness to receive whoever comes to him.

The new liturgical regulation and, more recently, the new Code of Canon Law (canons 961-963) specify the conditions which make it lawful to use "the rite of reconciliation of a number of penitents with general confession and absolution". The norms and regulations given on this point, which are the result of mature and balanced consideration, must be accepted and applied in such a way as to avoid any sort of arbitrary interpretation.

It is opportune to reflect more deeply on the reasons which order the celebration of Penance in one of the first two forms and permit the use of the third form. First of all, there is the reason of fidelity to the will of the Lord Jesus, transmitted by the doctrine of the Church and also the reason of obedience to the Church's laws. The Synod repeated in one of its *Propositiones* the unchanged teaching which the Church has derived from the most ancient tradition, and it repeated the law with which she has codified the ancient penitential practice: the individual and integral confession of sins with individual absolution constitutes the only ordinary way in which the faithful who are conscious of serious sin are reconciled with God and with the Church. From this confirmation of the Church's teaching it is clear that every serious sin must always be stated, with its determining circumstances, in an individual confession.

Then there is a reason of the pastoral order. While it is true that, when the conditions required by canonical discipline occur, use may be made of the third form of celebration, it must not be forgotten that this form cannot become an ordinary one, and it cannot and must not be used - as the Synod repeated - except "in cases of grave necessity". And there remains unchanged the obligation to make an individual confession of serious sins before again having recourse to another general absolution. The Bishop therefore, who is the only one competent in his own diocese to assess whether the conditions actually exist which Canon Law lays down for the use of the third form, will give this judgement with a grave obligation on his own conscience, with full respect for the law and practice of the Church, and also taking into account the criteria and guidelines agreed upon - on the basis of the doctrinal and pastoral considerations explained above - with the other members of the Episcopal Conference. Equally, it will always be a matter of genuine pastoral concern to lay down and guarantee the conditions that make recourse to the third form capable of producing the spiritual fruits for which it is meant. The exceptional use of the third form of celebration must never lead to a lesser regard for, still less an abandonment of, the ordinary forms, nor must it lead to this form being considered an alternative to the other two forms. It is not in fact left to the freedom of pastors and the faithful to choose from among these forms the one considered most suitable. It remains the obligation of pastors to facilitate for the faithful the practice of integral and individual confession of sin, which constitutes for them not only a duty but also an inviolable and inalienable right, besides being something needed by the soul. For the faithful the use of the third form of celebration involves the obligation of following all the norms regulating its exercise, including that of not having recourse again to general absolution before a normal integral and individual confession of sins, which must be made as soon as possible. Before granting absolution the priest must inform and instruct the faithful about this norm and about the obligation to observe it.

With this reminder of the doctrine and the law of the Church I wish to instil into everyone the lively sense of responsibility which must guide us when we deal with sacred things like the Sacraments, which are not our property, or like consciences, which have a right not to be left in uncertainty and confusion. The Sacraments and consciences, I repeat, are sacred, and both require that we serve them in truth.

This is the reason for the Church's law.

I consider it my duty to mention at this point, if very briefly, a pastoral case that the Synod dealt with - in so far as it was able to do so - and which it also considered in one of the *Propositiones*. I am referring to certain situations, not infrequent today, affecting Christians who wish to continue their sacramental religious practice but who are prevented from doing so by their personal condition, which is not in harmony with the commitments freely undertaken before God and the Church. These are situations which seem particularly delicate and almost inextricable.

On this matter, which also deeply torments our pastoral hearts, it seemed my precise duty to say clear words in the Apostolic Exhortation *Familiaris Consortio* (no. 84), as regards the case of the divorced and remarried, and likewise the case of Christians living together in an irregular union.

At the same time, and together with the Synod, I feel that it is my clear duty to urge the ecclesial communities, and especially the bishops, to provide all possible assistance to those priests who have fallen short of the grave commitments which they undertook at their ordination and who are living in irregular situations. None of these brothers of ours should feel abandoned by the Church.

For all those who are not at the present moment in the objective conditions required by the Sacrament of Penance, the Church's manifestations of maternal kindness, the support of acts of piety apart from sacramental ones, a sincere effort to maintain contact with the Lord, attendance at Mass, and the frequent repetition of acts of faith, hope, charity and sorrow made as perfectly as possible can prepare the way for full reconciliation at the hour that Providence alone knows.

I entrust to the Father, rich in mercy, I entrust to the Son of God, made man as our Redeemer and Reconciler, I entrust to the Holy Spirit, source of unity and peace, this call of mine, as father and pastor, to penance and reconciliation. May the Most Holy Adorable Trinity cause to spring up in the Church and in the world the small seed which at this hour I plant in the generous soil of many human hearts.

In order that in the not too distant future abundant fruits may come from it, I invite you all to join me in turning to Christ's Heart, the eloquent sign of the divine mercy, the "propitiation for our sins", "our peace and reconciliation" (Litany of the Sacred Heart), that we may draw from it an interior encouragement to hate sin and to be converted to God, and find in it the divine kindness which lovingly responds to human repentance.

I likewise invite you to turn with me to the Immaculate Heart of Mary, Mother of Jesus, in whom "is effected the reconciliation of God with humanity..., is accomplished the work of reconciliation, because she has received from God the fullness of grace in virtue of the redemptive sacrifice of Christ" (Audience Address, 7 December 1983). Truly, Mary has been associated with God, by virtue of her divine Motherhood, in the work of reconciliation.

Into the hands of this Mother, whose *fiat* marked the beginning of that "fullness of time" in which Christ accomplished the reconciliation of humanity with God, to her Immaculate Heart - to which we have repeatedly entrusted the whole of humanity, disturbed by sin and tormented by so many tensions and conflicts - I now in a special way entrust this intention: that through her intercession humanity may discover and travel the path of penance, the only path that can lead it to full reconciliation.

O.R. 865   17 December 1984

INDEX